TIME PASSAGES

By Robert Burtt & Bill Main

"The key to unlocking the door to our future opens with a journey into the past."

FIRST PRINTING

President Harry S. Truman delivers his "State Of The Union" address in Washington, D.C.

Sunday	Monday	Tuesday	Wednesday	Thursday	Friday	Saturday

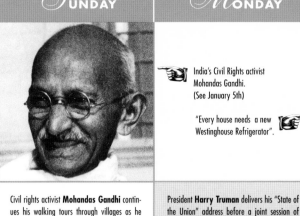

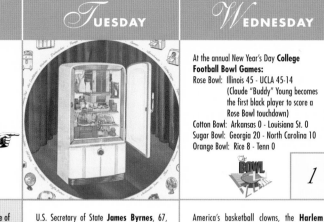

Monday

 India's Civil Rights activist Mohandas Gandhi. (See January 5th)

 "Every house needs a new Westinghouse Refrigerator".

Tuesday

At the annual New Year's Day **College Football Bowl Games:**
Rose Bowl: Illinois 45 - UCLA 45-14 (Claude "Buddy" Young becomes the first black player to score a Rose Bowl touchdown)
Cotton Bowl: Arkansas 0 - Louisiana St. 0
Sugar Bowl: Georgia 20 - North Carolina 10
Orange Bowl: Rice 8 - Tenn 0 **1**

Wednesday

From The Hit Parade:
The #1 song this week is "(I Love You) For Sentimental Reasons" by Nat King Cole.

Doubleday publishes **"Lydia Bailey"**, written by Kenneth Robert. It is the Liberty Guild's "Selection of the Month". **2**

Thursday

The **80th U.S. Congress** convenes with Republicans holding a majority for the first time since 1931. The seating immediately erupts in an uproar as Senator Glen Taylor of Idaho proposes that Senator Theodore Bilbo of Mississippi be barred, pending an investigation into whether he used intimidation to keep blacks from voting. **3**

Friday

Author Somerset Maugham's **"The Razor's Edge"**, becomes the all-time best-selling novel having sold more than 3 million copies. The novel has now sold more copies than Margaret Mitchell's "Gone with the Wind". **4**

Civil rights activist **Mohandas Gandhi** continues his walking tours through villages as he attempts to improve Hindu-Moslem relations in India. Just over a year from now (January 30th, 1948) Gandhi will be assassinated by a fanatic opposed to his peace-seeking ideas and methods. **5**

President **Harry Truman** delivers his "State of the Union" address before a joint session of Congress. Having to deal with a Republican-dominated Congress, Truman starts by saying *"the power to mold the future of this nation lies in our hands - yours and mine"*.

Ben Hogan wins the $10,000 L.A. Open. **6**

U.S. Secretary of State **James Byrnes**, 67, resigns after serving for 18 months, citing illness as his reason for stepping down. President Truman nominates General George C. Marshall, 66, to succeed him.

Manuel Ortiz loses his World Bantamweight Boxing crown to Harold Dade, 23, in a 15-round decision. **7**

America's basketball clowns, the **Harlem Globetrotters** begin their 21st season, coached by their founder, Abraham Saperstein.

Elvis Presley celebrates his 12th birthday.

Future rock star **David Bowie** is born "David Jones" in Brixton, England. **8**

Harvard University demonstrates its new Mark II super-powered **calculating machine**, capable of solving detailed multiplication problems in a second. The machine will be used by the Navy to assist in solving ballistic missile problems. Professor Howard Aiken led in the breakthrough machine's construction. **9**

The Broadway musical **"Finian's Rainbow"**, opens at the 46 St. Theater in New York City, featuring Albert Sharpe, David Wayne, Ella Logan, Donald Richards and Anita Alvarez. Written by E.Y. Harburg and Fred Saldy, the lyrics are by Harburg with the music by Burton Lawe. The musical will run for 723 performances closing on October 2nd, 1948.
BROADWAY **10**

ABC-Radio introduces a new program, **"Murder and Mrs. Malone"**, starring Frank Lovejoy.

Baseball great **Honus Wagner** signs a contract to coach the Pittsburgh Pirates. During his 21-year playing career, Wagner had a career hitting .321 average. **11**

The first **all-black programming** radio station begins service in Memphis, Tennessee. Later this year, the first all-Spanish U.S. radio station will begin broadcasting in San Antonio.

An Eastern Airlines plane en route from Detroit to Miami **crashes during a severe rain storm** near Galax, Florida, killing 18 of the 19 people aboard. **12**

A U.S. Supreme Court rules 5-4 that the State of Louisiana may once again order the **execution** of convicted murderer Willie Francis, who survived a previous execution attempt when the electric chair he was to be executed in malfunctioned. **13**

Convicted Nazi doctor Hilde Werdicke and nurse Helene Wieczorek, who injected death serum into hundreds of mentally unstable patients in a Nazi hospital, are **guillotined** in Berlin's Lehrterstrasse Prison.

Actress **Gene Tierney** files for a divorce from husband Count Oleg Cassini. **14**

Ford Motor President **Henry Ford II**, 29, announces plans to reduce passenger-car prices by up to $20 in an attempt to help stem the dramatic inflationary trends in the United States that began following the end of World War II.
AUTO INDUSTRY
 Mrs. Eleanor Roosevelt's driver's license is routinely revoked following her involvement in an accident during 1946. **15**

Vietnam Republic leader **Ho Chi Minh** announces that Vietnam will not stop fighting until their independence has been achieved. The French continue to occupy Haiphong, refusing to negotiate. **16**

The NFL champion Chicago Cardinals sign former Georgia college halfback **Charley Tripi** to a 4-year contract worth $100,000. **17**

The #1 song on the **Country & Western Music Chart** is "Rainbow At Midnight" by Ernest Tubb.

Detroit Tigers home-run leader **Henry "Hank" Greenberg** is sold to the Pittsburgh Pirates. On February 21st, Greenberg will sign for a sum reported to be higher than the $55,000 he was receiving from Detroit. **18**

A tragic **marine disaster** occurs as a Greek steamer, named the "Himara" hits a World War II mine off the coast of Athens, Greece, killing 392 of the almost 700 people who are aboard the liner.

George Schoux, 28, wins the $10,000 Richmond, California Golf Tournament. **19**

Josh Gibson, 38, dies. Gibson, who had retired from the Negro Baseball League, is credited with 960 home runs during his 17-year career. Due to inconsistent record-keeping, it is widely believed he has actually hit many more. **20**

Motorists are paying an average of 23¢ per **gallon of gasoline** this year to fuel their automobiles.

Teachers in N.Y. State receive a $300 increase. The **teacher's minimum salary is now $2,000 a year.** **21**

The first commercial television station west of the Mississippi River, **KTLA** begins operations in Hollywood, California.

President Truman asks **Herbert Hoover** to undertake a fact-finding mission to Austria and Germany to better understand the food and monetary issues that are causing massive relief tax burdens to U.S. taxpayers. **22**

Government officials in Canada cancel plans to **deport Japanese-Canadians** after a large protest by Liberal politicians sways their actions. During World War II, over 20,000 Japanese-Canadians had been forced into detention centers. Close to 10,500 Japanese have already accepted financial assistance to return to Japan. **23**

A major labor agreement is reached between the **United Steelworkers and U.S. Steel**, providing new pay ranges up to a maximum of $1.98 an hour for skilled workers. Employees will receive the pay increase retroactive to 1944.

Actor Dean Jagger is barred from obtaining a license to marry Gloria Ling. A California State law forbids marriages between Caucasians and Mongolians. Ling's father is from China. **24**

Alphonse Capone, better known as **"Big Al Scarface"** Capone, 48, dies on his family estate in Miami. Capone, who led gangsters in Chicago during the 1920s, dies after a long battle with syphilis. Capone ended up going to jail on a tax evasion conviction in 1932, and was transferred to the Alcatraz maximum security prison when it opened in 1934. **25**

ABC-Radio introduces a new program **"The Greatest Story Ever Told"**. It is the first radio program to portray the voice of Jesus.

A KLM airliner crashes during takeoff from Kastrup Airport in Copenhagen, killing all 22 aboard, including American opera, radio and screen star Grace Moore, 45, along with Prince Gustav Adolf, 40, who is second in line to the Swedish throne. **26**

The **Australian Tennis Championships** in Sydney conclude with Dinny Pails winning the Men's Singles title over last year's winner, John Bromwich 4-6, 6-4, 3-6, 7-5, 8-6. The Women's Singles title is won for the third straight time by Nancye Wynne Bolton who defeats Nell Hopman 6-3, 6-2. **27**

At a New York auction, the first known book printed in the English colonies in America, **"The Bay Psalm Book"**, is sold for a record $151,000.

A Japanese carpenter attacks **General Douglas MacArthur** with a wooden sword. After MacArthur disarms the man, he says he chose the dramatic method to present a written plea for Japan which was attached to the sword. **28**

The new Broadway play **"All My Sons"**, opens at the Coronet Theater in New York City, starring Ted Begley, Beth Merrill, Arthur Kennedy and Lois Wheeler. The play, written by Arthur Miller, will run until November 8th with 328 consecutive performances. The "Billboard" poll of theatrical professionals will choose the play as the Best Play of the 1946-1947 season.
BROADWAY **29**

A series of **tornadoes** roll across the states of Missouri, Arkansas, Georgia, Tennessee and Alabama, taking 21 lives.

Former war correspondent David L. Cohn looks at the world in his nonfiction book **"This is the Story"**, published by Houghton Mifflin. **30**

Officials in Yugoslavia formally **accuse the Vatican** of assisting alleged Yugoslav war criminals that escape following WWII. **31**

 1947 Mercury

 Singer Sewing Centers new portable sewing machine and folding travel irons.

 General Electric clocks (Top To Bottom)
The Adams - $535
The Ridgefield - $32
The Rhapsody - $55

"Charlie McCarthy" with ventriloquist *Edgar Bergan* continues to be one of America's favorite radio programs.

Sunday	Monday	Tuesday	Wednesday	Thursday	Friday	Saturday

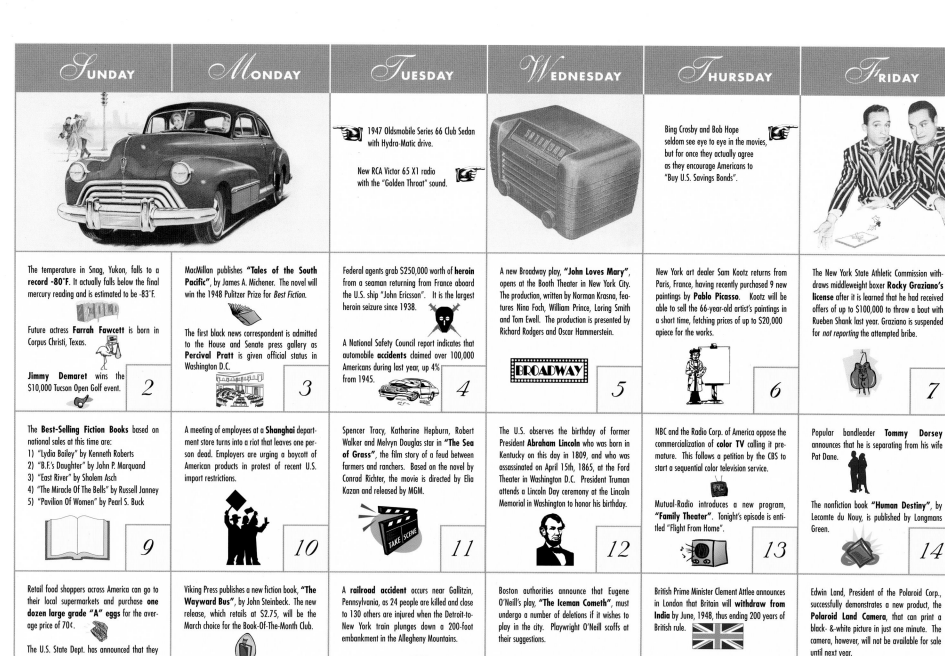

(Sunday — top) 1947 Oldsmobile Series 66 Club Sedan with Hydra-Matic drive.

(Tuesday — top) 1947 Oldsmobile Series 66 Club Sedan with Hydra-Matic drive.

New RCA Victor 65 X1 radio with the "Golden Throat" sound.

(Wednesday — top) (radio image)

(Thursday — top) Bing Crosby and Bob Hope seldom see eye to eye in the movies, but for once they actually agree as they encourage Americans to "Buy U.S. Savings Bonds".

(Saturday — top)  The network Hooperatings list the most popular radio shows at this time:
1) Bob Hope
2) Fibber McGee and Molly
3) Charlie McCarthy Show
4) Jack Benny
5) Fred Allen

1

---

2 (Sunday) The temperature in Snag, Yukon, falls to a **record -80°F**. It actually falls below the final mercury reading and is estimated to be -83°F.

Future actress **Farrah Fawcett** is born in Corpus Christi, Texas.

Jimmy Demaret wins the $10,000 Tucson Open Golf event.

3 (Monday) MacMillan publishes **"Tales of the South Pacific"**, by James A. Michener. The novel will win the 1948 Pulitzer Prize for *Best Fiction*.

The first black news correspondent is admitted to the House and Senate press gallery as **Percival Pratt** is given official status in Washington D.C.

4 (Tuesday) Federal agents grab $250,000 worth of **heroin** from a seaman returning from France aboard the U.S. ship "John Ericsson". It is the largest heroin seizure since 1938.

A National Safety Council report indicates that automobile **accidents** claimed over 100,000 Americans during last year, up 4% from 1945.

5 (Wednesday) A new Broadway play, **"John Loves Mary"**, opens at the Booth Theater in New York City. The production, written by Norman Krasna, features Nina Foch, William Prince, Loring Smith and Tom Ewell. The production is presented by Richard Rodgers and Oscar Hammerstein.

BROADWAY

6 (Thursday) New York art dealer Sam Kootz returns from Paris, France, having recently purchased 9 new paintings by **Pablo Picasso**. Kootz will be able to sell the 66-year-old artist's paintings in a short time, fetching prices of up to $20,000 apiece for the works.

7 (Friday) The New York State Athletic Commission withdraws middleweight boxer **Rocky Graziano's license** after it is learned that he had received offers of up to $100,000 to throw a bout with Rueben Shank last year. Graziano is suspended for *not reporting* the attempted bribe.

8 (Saturday) **From The Hit Parade:**
The #1 song this week is **"Huggin' and Chalkin'"** by Hoagy Carmichel with The Chickadees.

The #1 song on the Country & Western Music Chart is **"So Round, So Firm, So Fully Packed"** by Merle Travis. In 1946, Travis also hit #1 with his song "Divorce Me C.O.D.".

---

9 (Sunday) The **Best-Selling Fiction Books** based on national sales at this time are:
1) "Lydia Bailey" by Kenneth Roberts
2) "B.F.'s Daughter" by John P. Marquand
3) "East River" by Sholem Asch
4) "The Miracle Of The Bells" by Russell Janney
5) "Pavilion Of Women" by Pearl S. Buck

10 (Monday) A meeting of employees at a **Shanghai** department store turns into a riot that leaves one person dead. Employers are urging a boycott of American products in protest of recent U.S. import restrictions.

11 (Tuesday) Spencer Tracy, Katharine Hepburn, Robert Walker and Melvyn Douglas star in **"The Sea of Grass"**, the film story of a feud between farmers and ranchers. Based on the novel by Conrad Richter, the movie is directed by Elia Kazan and released by MGM.

12 (Wednesday) The U.S. observes the birthday of former President **Abraham Lincoln** who was born in Kentucky on this day in 1809, and who was assassinated on April 15th, 1865, at the Ford Theater in Washington D.C. President Truman attends a Lincoln Day ceremony at the Lincoln Memorial in Washington to honor his birthday.

13 (Thursday) NBC and the Radio Corp. of America oppose the commercialization of **color TV** calling it premature. This follows a petition by the CBS to start a sequential color television service.

Mutual-Radio introduces a new program, **"Family Theater"**. Tonight's episode is entitled "Flight From Home".

14 (Friday) Popular bandleader **Tommy Dorsey** announces that he is separating from his wife Pat Dane.

The nonfiction book **"Human Destiny"**, by Lecomte du Nouy, is published by Longmans Green.

15 (Saturday) The worst **commercial airliner crash** to date occurs when a Colombian Airlines DC-4 crashes into the side of Mt. Tablazo near Bogota, taking the lives of all 53 aboard.

Tommy Quinn wins the Baxter Mile Run in N.Y. with a time of 4:17.7.

---

16 (Sunday) Retail food shoppers across America can go to their local supermarkets and purchase **one dozen large grade "A" eggs** for the average price of 70¢.

The U.S. State Dept. has announced that they will begin easing **travel restrictions** to Europe to those who have proof of return passage, committed lodging, and food arrangements.

17 (Monday) Viking Press publishes a new fiction book, **"The Wayward Bus"**, by John Steinbeck. The new release, which retails at $2.75, will be the March choice for the Book-Of-The-Month Club.

A mob kidnaps black **Willie Earle**, 25, (arrested in a stabbing) from a North Carolina jail and lynch him.

18 (Tuesday) A **railroad accident** occurs near Gallitzin, Pennsylvania, as 24 people are killed and close to 130 others are injured when the Detroit-to-New York train plunges down a 200-foot embankment in the Allegheny Mountains.

19 (Wednesday) Boston authorities announce that Eugene O'Neill's play, **"The Iceman Cometh"**, must undergo a number of deletions if it wishes to play in the city. Playwright O'Neill scoffs at their suggestions.

BROADWAY

20 (Thursday) British Prime Minister Clement Attlee announces in London that Britain will **withdraw from India** by June, 1948, thus ending 200 years of British rule.

A chemical explosion at the **O'Connor Electroplating Company** in L.A. takes out close to 5 blocks, killing 15 people while injuring 160 others.

21 (Friday) Edwin Land, President of the Polaroid Corp., successfully demonstrates a new product, the **Polaroid Land Camera**, that can print a black- & -white picture in just one minute. The camera, however, will not be available for sale until next year.

22 (Saturday) Former New York Vice King, **Charles "Lucky" Luciano**, who was deported to Italy in 1946, is arrested in Havana, Cuba (where he recently established himself), and is asked to leave. The U.S. threatens to cut off Cuba's supply of narcotic drugs fearing Luciano would get hold of them for illegal use.

Simon & Schuster publishes the fiction book **"Gentlemen's Agreement"** by Laura Hobson.

---

23 (Sunday) One of the most popular songs in the U.S. during this time is **"Zip-A-Dee Doo Dah"** by Ray Gilbert and Allie Wrubel. The song is well known from its inclusion in the Walt Disney movie "Song of the South".

24 (Monday) The largest **teachers strike** in U.S. history begins in Buffalo, New York, as 2,400 teachers walk out demanding significant pay increases. At present, elementary teachers earn between $1,175-$2,575 a year, while high school teachers earn up to $2,975. The strike will end March 3rd when raises up to $675 per year will be accepted.

25 (Tuesday) **From The Hit Parade:**
Freddy Martin's hit song "Managua, Nicaragua" is the #1 single this week.

The story of the development of the atomic bomb is told in the MGM film **"The Beginning Of The End"**, starring Brian Donlevy, Robert Walker and Beverly Tyler.

26 (Wednesday) President Truman sends to Congress a draft of a bill to **unify the armed services**. All three branches will have equal status under a civilian Secretary of Cabinet rank.

The book **"Citizen Tom Paine"**, by Howard Fast is banned from schools in N.Y. for *"objectionable passages"*.

27 (Thursday) Former President Herbert Hoover, on return from his European task force mission, reports that both the U.S. and Great Britain must contribute **food rations** for German civilians located within their zones. Hoover, assigned by Truman, reports widespread German malnutrition which must be overcome first if Germany is ever going to begin reconstruction.

28 (Friday) World Light-Heavyweight Boxing Champ **Gus Lesnevich** retains his title knocking out Billy Fox in the 10th round during their bout in L.A.

The former Prince of Greece, 6th in line to the throne, **Lt. Philip Mountbatten**, 26, becomes a British subject, giving up his title and claims to the Greek throne. It is speculated he will soon become engaged to Princess Elizabeth.

(Saturday — bottom)  **Me for CRUSH**

Orange Crush "Served ice cold from the dispenser".

(Bottom row)

Spencer Tracy and Katharine Hepburn star in the new film "The Sea Of Grass". (See February 11th)

Sunbeam's new Mixmaster & juice extractor.

MARCH *1947*

The film "The Best Years Of Our Lives" dominates the Academy Award "Oscar" presentations.

SUNDAY	MONDAY	TUESDAY	WEDNESDAY	THURSDAY	FRIDAY	SATURDAY

1947 Studebaker Commander Regal DeLuxe Coupe. "First by far with a postwar car".

Claude Jarman Jr. wins the "Best Juvenile Actor" Oscar for his role in the film "The Yearling". (See March 13th)

Jack Kramer & Pauline Betz celebrate their wins at the National Indoor Tennis Championships. (See March 8th)

1

The new hit song **"Open The Door Richard"** by Clinton Fletcher, John Mason, Dan Howell and Jack McVea is sweeping the nation. Close to 500,000 copies of the skit-based song have reportedly now been sold.

2

Pope Pius XII celebrates his 71st birthday in Rome. On March 12th, the Pope will begin the 9th year of his reign.

The first **concentrated frozen orange** juice from Florida is now available in northern U.S. stores.

3

A new Broadway play, **"The Importance Of Being Earnest"** opens at the Royale Theater in New York City. Written by Oscar Wilde, the play is staged by John Gielgud who also stars with Margaret Rutherford, Pamela Brown, Jane Baxter, Robert Flemyng, Jean Cadell and John Kidd.

BROADWAY

4

The #1 song on the Country & Western Music Chart **is "Besame Mucho"** by Jimmy Dorsey.

U.S. Commander in South Korea **Lt. General John Hodge tells the press**, *"I believe that when the Russians believe we are not out to take over the world...they will work with us".*

5

Elia Kazan directs the dramatic murder trial film based on a true incident in **"Boomerang!"**, starring Dana Andrews, Jane Wyatt, Lee J. Cobb, Cara Williams, Arthur Kennedy, Sam Levene, Ed Begley and Karl Malden. Released by 20th Century-Fox.

ADMIT ONE

6

The House votes to restore former President **Hoover's name to Boulder Dam**. Democratic Interior Secretary Harold Ickes changed the name in 1933.

The U.S. Supreme Court rules 7-2 that John L. Lewis and the **United Mine Workers** were in criminal contempt of court when they went on strike last November at the government-operated coal mines.

7

A British Navy court martial orders **Lt. John Wardle** dismissed from his ship, reprimanded, and his seniority reduced by 3 months. Wardle's crime was that he ate Christmas dinner with 5 enlisted men aboard a mine sweeper. They were the only ones aboard.

8

National Indoor Tennis Championships:
Men's Singles: Jack Kramer defeats Bob Falkenburg 6-1, 6-2, 6-2
Women's Singles: Pauline Betz defeats Doris Hart 6-2, 7-5

Dick Button retains the U.S. Men's Figure Skating title in Berkeley, California.

9

Ronald Colman and Peggy Cummins star in the film version of the John P. Marquand & George S. Kaufman play, **"The Late George Apley"**. The satirical movie look at Boston's blue-blooded families is directed by Joseph L. Mankiewicz.

Gretchen Merrill wins the U.S. Women's Figure Skating title in Berkeley, CA.

10

Future rock star **Tom Scholtz** is born in Toledo, Ohio. Scholtz will go on to lead the popular rock group "Boston". Their self-titled album "Boston" will sell an incredible 2.7 million copies in just 7 months with two #1 hit singles "More Than A Feeling" and "Long Time".

11

Children that are fortunate enough to have a television can now the new TV program, **"The Small Fry Club"**. The show stars *"Honey The Bunny"* and *"Peppy The Penguin"* and is hosted by Bob Emery.

12

President Harry Truman **addresses a joint session of Congress** outlining a doctrine intended to control Communism. At the same session, he asks Congress to appropriate $400 million for the aid of Turkey and Greece to begin their anti-Communism crusade.

13

The 19th **Academy Awards** (Oscars) include:
Best Picture: "The Best Years Of Our Lives"
Director: William Wyler "The Best Years ..."
Actress: Olivia de Havilland "To Each His Own"
Actor: Frederic March "The Best Years ..."
Juvenile Actor: Claude Jarman Jr. "The Yearling"
Supp Actress: Anne Baxter "The Razor's Edge"
Supp Actor: Harold Russell "The Best Years ..."

HOLLYWOOD MOVIES

14

A 99-year **treaty** is signed by the United States and Philippine governments which guarantees the U.S. military and naval bases on the islands. President Manuel Roxas and U.S. Ambassador Paul McNutt sign the treaty.

Treaty

15

Radio game-show contestant, Mrs. William McCormick of Pennsylvania, wins close to $18,000 worth of prizes, including a new car, as she correctly identifies a mystery voice on NBC's **"Truth or Consequences"** as retired actress Clare Bow. During 1945, "Truth or Consequences" began the Mystery Guest portion of the show. The program is hosted by Ralph Edwards.

16

Sources estimate that close to 13 million Americans tune their radios to hear the radio singing debut of **Margaret Truman**, 23, as she performs with the Detroit Symphony.

It is estimated that less than 50% of all Americans **use toothbrushes.**

17

The United States announces plans to set up **soup kitchens in Germany** to feed 3.5 million children and 1 million seniors, as recommended by Former President Herbert Hoover in his task force report.

18

The **CBS Broadcasting Network** receives a setback when the FCC rules against the commercial use of CBS's mechanical color television, ruling that it would be better served to expand black-&-white video until color is developed further.

19

CBS-Radio's **"Your Hit Parade"** ranks "Anniversary Song" by Al Jolson and Saul Chaplin as the #1 song. Other hits include "Managua Nicaragua" by Albert Gamse and Irving Fields and "For Sentimental Reasons" by Deek Watson & William Best.

The Public Land Commission approves a bill to make **Hawaii** a U.S. state.

HAWAII

20

Loretta Young plays a Swedish country girl who comes to the big city in the film **"The Farmer's Daughter"**. Released by RKO, the movie also stars Joseph Cotten, Ethel Barrymore, Charles Bickford and Harry Davenport.

Pope Pius XII appeals for worldwide **contributions to rebuild Monte Cassino Abbey** which was destroyed during WWII.

21

The Alan Jay Lerner and Frederick Loewe musical **"Brigadoon"** is playing in its second week at the Ziegfeld Theater in New York City. Staged by Robert Lewis, the musical features David Brooks, Marion Bell, Pamela Britton, Lee Sullivan, George Keane, William Hansen and James Mitchell. It will enjoy a run of 581 performances.

BROADWAY

22

Bobby Riggs wins the **World Pro Indoor Tennis Championship** over Don Budge 6-1, 8-6, 6-3 in Philadelphia. Riggs & Budge defeat Fred Perry & Frank Kovaks 6-2, 6-8, 6-1, 4-6, 6-3 to capture the doubles title .

"Armed", with jockey Doug Dodgson aboard, wins the **Gulfstream Florida Handicap**.

23

NHL Final Standings:

	W	L	T	Pts
Montreal	34	16	10	78
Toronto	31	19	10	72
Boston	26	23	11	63
Detroit	22	27	11	55
New York	22	32	6	50
Chicago	19	37	4	42

24

Utah University defeats Kentucky University 49-45 to win the **NIT Collegiate Basketball Tournament** final in New York. The MVP award goes to Utah's center Vern Gardner who scored 15 points in the final, giving him a total of 51 points for the tournament.

25

Future singer **Elton John** is born as Reginald Dwight in Middlesex, England.

BIRTHS

The worst **mining disaster** in the U.S. since 1928, occurs in Centralia, Illinois, when 111 workers are killed.

The **NCAA basketball championship** is won by Holy Cross 58-47 over Oklahoma.

26

NHL Season Leaders:
Points: Max Bentley (Chicago) 72
Goals: Maurice Richard (Montreal) 45
Assists: Billy Taylor (Detroit) 46
Goals-Against Avg: Bill Durnan (Montreal) 2.3
Penalty Minutes: Gus Mortson (Toronto) 133

Canada ends **meat rationing.** The Government does however retain price controls.

27

The ***baby boom* years** are here as the Census Bureau reports that an all-time one-year record of 3,440,000 babies were born in the U.S. during 1946.

U.S. officials announce they are **hunting for Hitler's understudy** Martin Bormann, who was originally believed to have died on May 5th, 1945. Recent reports, however, suggest he is somewhere in Europe.

28

Former Chicago baseball star **Johnny Evers**, 65, dies in Albany, New York. Evers will long be remembered as the second baseman in the famous "Tinker to Evers to Chance" double-play combination.

The last episode of the popular radio program **"Buck Rogers in the Twenty-Fifth Century"** airs on the Mutual Network.

29

Chicago preacher **Gilbert Dodds** runs the season's fastest indoor mile with a time of 4:06.8. Dodds is coming off victories in Hamilton, Ontario, on March 22nd, Montreal, Quebec, on March 24th and Cleveland, Ohio, on March 18th. The Track Writers Association in New York will vote Dodds as the season's top indoor performer, on April 7th.

30

NBA Season Leaders:
Scoring: Joe Fulks (Phil) 1,389, 23.2 average
Assists: Ernie Calverly (Prov) 202
Free Throw Percentage: Fred Scolari (Wash) 81.1%

31

Professional Basketball Association Of America (BAA) Final Standings:

East	W	L	West	W	L
Wash.	49	11	Chic.	38	22
Phil.	35	25	St.L.	38	22
NY	33	27	Clev.	30	30
Prov.	28	32	Det.	20	40
Bost.	22	28	Pitts.	15	45
Tor.	22	38			

Joseph Cotton and Loretta Young star in the new film "The Farmer's Daughter". (See March 20th)

Stetson hats for both men & women. (L to R)
The "Flagship" $12.50
The "Westport" $14.95
The "Kashmir" $10

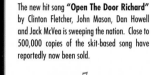

TIME · PASSAGES

A P R I L

1947

Jackie Robinson breaks the Major League Baseball color barrier playing for the Brooklyn Dodgers.

SUNDAY	MONDAY	TUESDAY	WEDNESDAY	THURSDAY	FRIDAY	SATURDAY

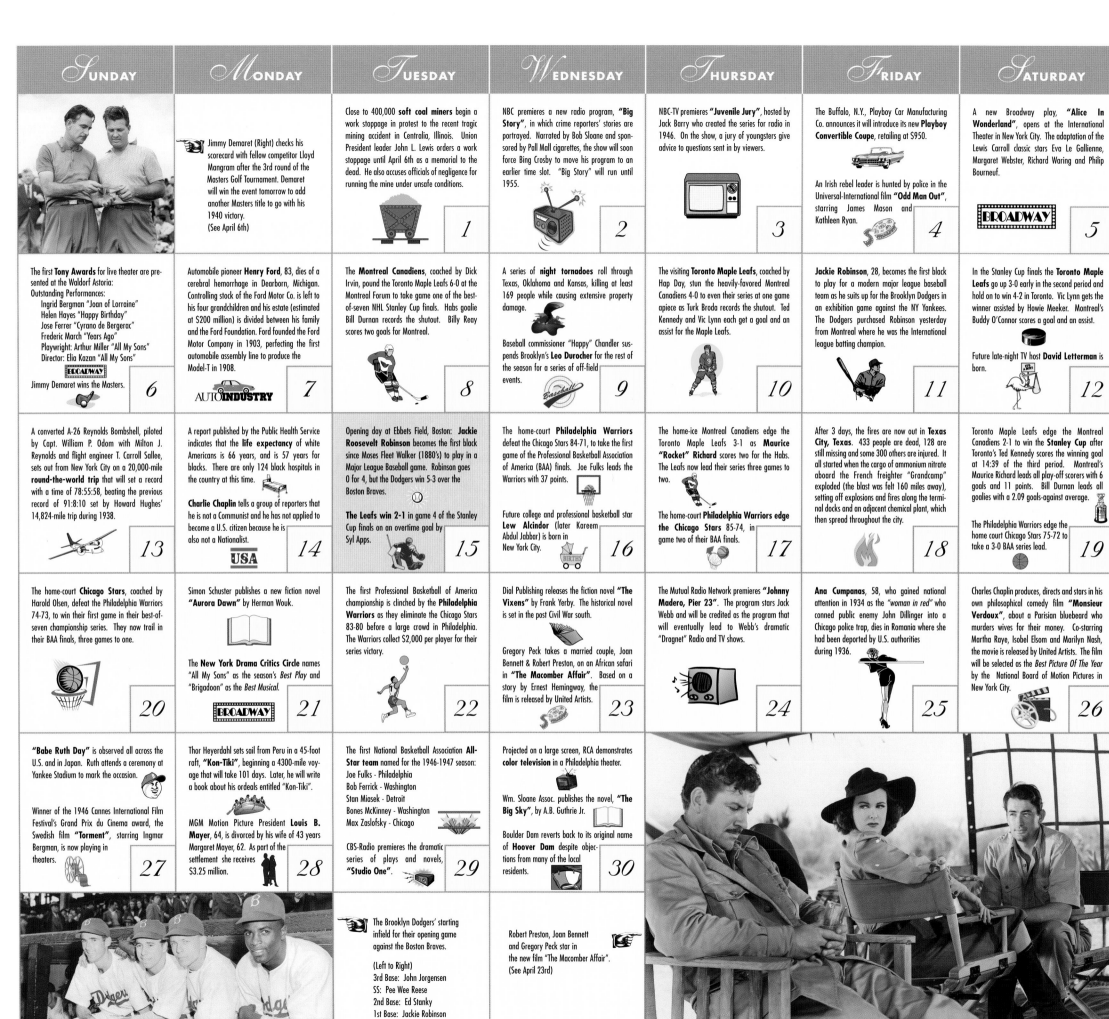

Monday (intro box): Jimmy Demaret (Right) checks his scorecard with fellow competitor Lloyd Mangram after the 3rd round of the Masters Golf Tournament. Demaret will win the event tomorrow to add another Masters title to go with his 1940 victory. (See April 6th)

Tuesday 1: Close to 400,000 soft coal miners begin a work stoppage in protest to the recent tragic mining accident in Centralia, Illinois. Union President leader John L. Lewis orders a work stoppage until April 6th as a memorial to the dead. He also accuses officials of negligence for running the mine under unsafe conditions.

Wednesday 2: NBC premieres a new radio program, **"Big Story"**, in which crime reporters' stories are portrayed. Narrated by Bob Sloane and sponsored by Pall Mall cigarettes, the show will soon force Bing Crosby to move his program to an earlier time slot. "Big Story" will run until 1955.

Thursday 3: NBC-TV premieres **"Juvenile Jury"**, hosted by Jack Barry who created the series for radio in 1946. On the show, a jury of youngsters give advice to questions sent in by viewers.

Friday 4: The Buffalo, N.Y., Playboy Car Manufacturing Co. announces it will introduce its new **Playboy Convertible Coupe**, retailing at $950.

An Irish rebel leader is hunted by police in the Universal-International film **"Odd Man Out"**, starring James Mason and Kathleen Ryan.

Saturday 5: A new Broadway play, **"Alice In Wonderland"**, opens at the International Theater in New York City. The adaptation of the Lewis Carroll classic stars Eva Le Gallienne, Margaret Webster, Richard Waring and Philip Bourneuf.

Sunday 6: The first **Tony Awards** for live theater are presented at the Waldorf Astoria:
Outstanding Performances:
Ingrid Bergman "Joan of Lorraine"
Helen Hayes "Happy Birthday"
Jose Ferrer "Cyrano de Bergerac"
Frederic March "Years Ago"
Playwright: Arthur Miller "All My Sons"
Director: Elia Kazan "All My Sons"
Jimmy Demaret wins the Masters.

Monday 7: Automobile pioneer **Henry Ford**, 83, dies of a cerebral hemorrhage in Dearborn, Michigan. Controlling stock of the Ford Motor Co. is left to his four grandchildren and his estate (estimated at $200 million) is divided between his family and the Ford Foundation. Ford founded the Ford Motor Company in 1903, perfecting the first automobile assembly line to produce the Model-T in 1908.

Tuesday 8: The **Montreal Canadiens**, coached by Dick Irvin, pound the Toronto Maple Leafs 6-0 at the Montreal Forum to take game one of the best-of-seven NHL Stanley Cup finals. Habs goalie Bill Durnan records the shutout. Billy Reay scores two goals for Montreal.

Wednesday 9: A series of **night tornadoes** roll through Texas, Oklahoma and Kansas, killing at least 169 people while causing extensive property damage.

Baseball commissioner "Happy" Chandler suspends Brooklyn's **Leo Durocher** for the rest of the season for a series of off-field events.

Thursday 10: The visiting **Toronto Maple Leafs**, coached by Hap Day, stun the heavily-favored Montreal Canadiens 4-0 to even their series at one game apiece as Turk Broda records the shutout. Ted Kennedy and Vic Lynn each get a goal and an assist for the Maple Leafs.

Friday 11: **Jackie Robinson**, 28, becomes the first black to play for a modern major league baseball team as he suits up for the Brooklyn Dodgers in an exhibition game against the NY Yankees. The Dodgers purchased Robinson yesterday from Montreal where he was the International league batting champion.

Saturday 12: In the Stanley Cup finals the **Toronto Maple Leafs** go up 3-0 early in the second period and hold on to win 4-2 in Toronto. Vic Lynn gets the winner assisted by Howie Meeker. Montreal's Buddy O'Connor scores a goal and an assist.

Future late-night TV host **David Letterman** is born.

Sunday 13: A converted A-26 Reynolds Bombshell, piloted by Capt. William P. Odom with Milton J. Reynolds and flight engineer T. Carroll Sallee, sets out from New York City on a 20,000-mile **round-the-world trip** that will set a record with a time of 78:55:58, beating the previous record of 91:8:10 set by Howard Hughes' 14,824-mile trip during 1938.

Monday 14: A report published by the Public Health Service indicates that the **life expectancy** of white Americans is 66 years, and is 57 years for blacks. There are only 124 black hospitals in the country at this time.

Charlie Chaplin tells a group of reporters that he is not a Communist and he has not applied to become a U.S. citizen because he is also not a Nationalist.

Tuesday 15: Opening day at Ebbets Field, Boston: **Jackie Roosevelt Robinson** becomes the first black since Moses Fleet Walker (1880's) to play in a Major League Baseball game. Robinson goes 0 for 4, but the Dodgers win 5-3 over the Boston Braves.

The Leafs win 2-1 in game 4 of the Stanley Cup finals on an overtime goal by Syl Apps.

Wednesday 16: The home-court **Philadelphia Warriors** defeat the Chicago Stars 84-71, to take the first game of the Professional Basketball Association of America (BAA) finals. Joe Fulks leads the Warriors with 37 points.

Future college and professional basketball star **Lew Alcindor** (later Kareem Abdul Jabbar) is born in New York City.

Thursday 17: The home-ice Montreal Canadiens edge the Toronto Maple Leafs 3-1 as **Maurice "Rocket" Richard** scores two for the Habs. The Leafs now lead their series three games to two.

The home-court **Philadelphia Warriors edge the Chicago Stars 85-74**, in game two of their BAA finals.

Friday 18: After 3 days, the fires are now out in **Texas City, Texas**. 433 people are dead, 128 are still missing and some 300 others are injured. It all started when the cargo of ammonium nitrate aboard the French freighter "Grandcamp" exploded (the blast was felt 160 miles away), setting off explosions and fires along the terminal docks and an adjacent chemical plant, which then spread throughout the city.

Saturday 19: Toronto Maple Leafs edge the Montreal Canadiens 2-1 to win the **Stanley Cup** after Toronto's Ted Kennedy scores the winning goal at 14:39 of the third period. Montreal's Maurice Richard leads all play-off scorers with 6 goals and 11 points. Bill Durnan leads all goalies with a 2.09 goals-against average.

The Philadelphia Warriors edge the home court Chicago Stars 75-72 to take a 3-0 BAA series lead.

Sunday 20: The home-court **Chicago Stars**, coached by Harold Olsen, defeat the Philadelphia Warriors 74-73, to win their first game in their best-of-seven championship series. They now trail in their BAA finals, three games to one.

Monday 21: Simon Schuster publishes a new fiction novel **"Aurora Dawn"** by Herman Wouk.

The **New York Drama Critics Circle** names "All My Sons" as the season's Best Play and "Brigadoon" as the Best Musical.

Tuesday 22: The first Professional Basketball of America championship is clinched by the **Philadelphia Warriors** as they eliminate the Chicago Stars 83-80 before a large crowd in Philadelphia. The Warriors collect $2,000 per player for their series victory.

Wednesday 23: Dial Publishing releases the fiction novel **"The Vixens"** by Frank Yerby. The historical novel is set in the post Civil War south.

Gregory Peck takes a married couple, Joan Bennett & Robert Preston, on an African safari in **"The Macomber Affair"**. Based on a story by Ernest Hemingway, the film is released by United Artists.

Thursday 24: The Mutual Radio Network premieres **"Johnny Madero, Pier 23"**. The program stars Jack Webb and will be credited as the program that will eventually lead to Webb's dramatic "Dragnet" Radio and TV shows.

Friday 25: **Ana Cumpanas**, 58, who gained national attention in 1934 as the "woman in red" who conned public enemy John Dillinger into a Chicago police trap, dies in Romania where she had been deported by U.S. authorities during 1936.

Saturday 26: Charles Chaplin produces, directs and stars in his own philosophical comedy film **"Monsieur Verdoux"**, about a Parisian bluebeard who murders wives for their money. Co-starring Martha Raye, Isobel Elsom and Marilyn Nash, the movie is released by United Artists. The film will be selected as the Best Picture Of The Year by the National Board of Motion Pictures in New York City.

Sunday 27: **"Babe Ruth Day"** is observed all across the U.S. and in Japan. Ruth attends a ceremony at Yankee Stadium to mark the occasion.

Winner of the 1946 Cannes International Film Festival's Grand Prix du Cinema award, the Swedish film **"Torment"**, starring Ingmar Bergman, is now playing in theaters.

Monday 28: Thor Heyerdahl sets sail from Peru in a 45-foot raft, **"Kon-Tiki"**, beginning a 4300-mile voyage that will take 101 days. Later, he will write a book about his ordeals entitled "Kon-Tiki".

MGM Motion Picture President **Louis B. Mayer**, 64, is divorced from his wife of 43 years Margaret Mayer, 62. As part of the settlement she receives $3.25 million.

Tuesday 29: The first National Basketball Association **All-Star team** named for the 1946-1947 season:
Joe Fulks - Philadelphia
Bob Ferrick - Washington
Stan Miasek - Detroit
Bones McKinney - Washington
Max Zaslofsky - Chicago

CBS-Radio premieres the dramatic series of plays and novels, **"Studio One"**.

Wednesday 30: Projected on a large screen, RCA demonstrates **color television** in a Philadelphia theater.

Wm. Sloane Assoc. publishes the novel, **"The Big Sky"**, by A.B. Guthrie Jr.

Boulder Dam reverts back to its original name of **Hoover Dam** despite objections from many of the local residents.

Bottom notes:

The Brooklyn Dodgers' starting infield for their opening game against the Boston Braves.

(Left to Right)
3rd Base: John Jorgensen
SS: Pee Wee Reese
2nd Base: Ed Stanky
1st Base: Jackie Robinson
(See April 15th & May 8th)

Robert Preston, Joan Bennett and Gregory Peck star in the new film "The Macomber Affair". (See April 23rd)

MAY

1947

Mauri Rose, seen here following a qualifying run, wins this year's "Indy 500".

Sunday	Monday	Tuesday	Wednesday	Thursday	Friday	Saturday
	Swimming sensation Ann Curtis clutches the stopwatch after setting a new American record time in the 100-yard Freestyle Swimming event at the AAU championships. (See May 2nd & 4th)	"Amos 'n' Andy" is one of the top radio programs on the air. (See May 13th)		**This Season's NHL All-Star Team:** Goal: Bill Durnan (Montreal) Defense: Emile Bouchard (Montreal) Ken Reardon (Montreal) Center: Milt Schmidt (Boston) Right Wing: Maurice Richard (Montreal) Left Wing: Doug Bentley (Chicago)	**Ann Curtis** sets a new American record of 59.4 seconds in a preliminary heat in the 100-yard freestyle swimming event at the AAU Championships. **Smallpox** continues to be a major health concern for Americans. In a major drive, over 6 million New Yorkers have now been vaccinated during the last three weeks. **2**	The chestnut colt "Jet Pilot" with jockey Eric Guerin aboard wins the 73rd **Kentucky Derby**, running the 1 1/4-mile distance in a time of 2:06 4/5, winning by a head over "Phalanx" to capture the $92,160 first prize. A $2.00 to win wager pays $12.80. "Faultless" finishes in third. The race record of 2:01 2/5 set in 1941 by "Whirlaway" remains intact. **3**
Ann Curtis leads her Crystal Plunge swimming team to victory in the National Women's Senior AAU championships in Seattle. Curtis sets 7 meet records, including a world record in the 440-yard freestyle event with a time of 5:07.9. Curtis ties for the individual honors with Nancy Merki. **4**	Columbia University announces the **Pulitzer Prize** winners for this year, including the *Best Editorial Cartoon* to "Chicago Daily News" Vaughn Shoemaker for his "Still Racing His Shadow" cartoon. As was the case in 1942 and 1944, no Pulitzer Prize for drama is awarded. Robert Penn Warren receives a Letters Pulitzer for his work "All The King's Men". **5**	American advertising agent Peter Hodgson buys a soft, elastic moldable substance from researchers at General Electric and, after repackaging, he will market a new product he calls **"Silly Putty"**. The children's toy product will become an instant success. **6**	NBC-TV premieres **"Kraft Television Theater"**. Tonight's episode is called "Double Door" starring John Baragrey. Considered to be a show that best exemplifies TV's Golden ERA, the "live drama" program will run until 1958 on both the NBC & ABC Networks. **7**	**President Truman** celebrates his 63rd birthday. Baseball's National League President, **Ford Frick** announces that St. Louis Cardinals officials have stopped a potential player strike against Jackie Robinson's playing with the Brooklyn Dodgers. Robinson's breaking of the color barrier has caused mixed reactions around the nation. **8**	**Harriet Lummis Smith**, best known for co-authoring the "Pollyanna" series, dies in Pennsylvania. Convicted killer **Willie Francis**, 18, dies in the electric chair at St. Martinsville, Louisiana. Francis earned notoriety in 1946, when he survived the electric chair, presumably because the chair malfunctioned. **9**	"Faultless", with jockey Doug Dodson aboard, wins the **Preakness Stakes** horse race for 3-year-olds, running the 1 3/16-mile distance in 1:59 flat. Second place goes to "On Trust" with "Phalanx" finishing third, in the historic race that was first run in 1873. **10**
The B.F. Goodrich Tire Company announces that it has developed a **tubeless tire**. South African golfer **Bobby Locke** wins the $10,000 Houston Open. **11**	Canadian Figure-Skating sensation **Barbara Ann Scott**, 19, returns a car she had been given by her fans in Ottawa, Canada. Scott returns the gift in order to retain her amateur status in order that she can compete in next year's Winter Olympic games in St. Moritz. Scott will win the Gold Medal at the 1948 Olympics. **12**	The NBC radio broadcasting network is enjoying strong ratings from the popular Tuesday night half-hour comedy **"Amos 'n' Andy"** program, starring Freeman Gosden as "Amos" and Charles J. Correll as "Andy". **From The Hit Parade:** The #1 song this week is "Linda" by Ray Noble and his Orchestra, featuring Buddy Clark. **13**	While meeting in Cincinnati, **segregation** is banned from union locals of the AFL Brotherhood of Railway and Steamship Clerks. Americans who invest their savings in local banks across the country this year receive **2.4% interest** on a regular savings account. **14**	The United Nations adjourns after its first Special Assembly at Flushing Meadows Park, New York, after approving the establishment of the 11-nation special inquiry committee on **Palestine** by a 46-7 vote. During the last two weeks, delegates have listened to many debates and recommendations regarding Palestine, including the Jewish demands for an independent state. **15**	A Texas District Judge rules against black student Herman Sweatt, who was **attempting to gain entrance into the law school** at the University of Texas. The Judge finds that segregation of white and black schools is required by the State of Texas Constitution. **Johnny Mize** sets a new National League record, scoring in his 16th consecutive game for the NY Giants. **16**	The battleship **"Oklahoma"**, originally sunk in Pearl Harbor during the 1941 Japanese attack, sinks while en route to San Francisco for salvage. British biochemist **Frederick Hopkins**, 86, dies. In 1906, Hopkins discovered vitamins. He received a Nobel Prize for Medicine in 1929. **17**
The #1 song on the **Country & Western Music Chart** is Red Foley's hit song "New Jolie Blonde (New Pretty Blonde)". In 1944, Foley also had a #1 hit when "Smoke on the Water" reached the top of the chart. **18**	The **Best-Selling Non-Fiction Books** in the U.S. at this time are: 1) "Peace Of Mind" by Joshua Loth Liebman 2) "Human Destiny" by Lecomte du Nouy 3) "A Study Of History" by Arnold J. Toynbee 4) "The Egg And I" by Betty MacDonald 5) "Information Please Almanac, 1947" **19**	The U.S. Army announces a ban on the use of **cigarettes** in army barter markets beginning June 1st. There is a growing concern that Germany is becoming a *"cigarette economy"*. Yesterday, the army banned private shipments of cigarettes to personnel stationed in Germany. An Army B-25 **crashes** in Illinois, killing 7. **20**	An **all-white jury** acquits all 28 defendants accused in the February 17th lynching of black Willie Earle, who was awaiting trial for a Pickens, South Carolina, stabbing of a taxi driver. The verdict was returned despite allegations that 26 of the 28 accused had confessed to their involvement in the lynching. **21**	Six NY Yankee players, including Joe DiMaggio, **have been fined** for not performing promotional obligations that they had agreed to in their contracts. It is believed Joe DiMaggio was fined $100. British actor **Laurence Olivier** celebrates his 40th birthday. *Happy Fortieth Birthday* **22**	Light-heavyweight boxing champ **Gus Lesnevich** sets a speed record for a knockout at a Madison Square Garden main event in New York City, when he knocks out heavyweight Melio Bettina in just 59 seconds of the first round. **23**	The 88th running of Canada's most prestigious horse race, **The King's Plate**, takes place in Toronto. North America's oldest continuously run stakes race is won by "Moldy", a 3-year-old bay gelding ridden by Colin McDonald. "Moldy's" owner, R.S. McLaughlin collects the purse valued at approximately $10,335. **24**
Future music star **Jessi Colter** is born in Phoenix, Arizona. In later years she will write one of the country's number one songs entitled "I'm Not Lisa, My Name Is Julie". Colter will marry Country-and-Western singing star Waylon Jennings in 1969. **25**	Great Britain's **Queen Mary** celebrates her 80th birthday. Wm. Sloan Association publishes the nonfiction book, **"Home Country"**, by Ernie Pyle. **26**	**The NHL Trophy Winners Include:** Hart (MVP): Maurice Richard, Montreal Art Ross (Scoring): Max Bentley, Chicago Vezina (Goalie): Bill Durnan, Montreal Calder (Rookie): Howie Meeker, Toronto Lady Byng (Sportsmanship): Bobby Bauer, Boston **27**	The famous Canadian **Dionne Quintuplets**, Yvonne, Cecile, Emile, Marie and Annette, of Callander, Ontario, became teenagers today. The quintuplets thrilled the world with their arrival in 1934 as the world's first-known surviving Quintuplets. The #1 song on the Country & Western Music Chart is Eddie Arnold's hit **"What is Life Without Love?"**. **28**	The U.S. Army completes two days of **executions** of 48 former Mauthausen concentration camp guards and torturers. It is the largest mass execution to date during the U.S. occupation in Germany. Wrestler **Lou Thesz** retains his World Wrestling title when challenger "Whipper" Billy Watson is disqualified for fouling during their match at Maple Leaf Gardens in Toronto. **29**	The 31st annual **Indianapolis 500** Memorial Day auto race is won by Mauri Rose of Chicago who takes the $25,000 first prize, with an average speed of 116.338 mph. Rose's second Indy win is marred when one of the 30 starters, Bill "Shorty" Cantlon, is killed after crashing into a wall. The INDY **30**	"Phalanx", with jockey Ruperto Donoso aboard, wins the 79th **Belmont Stakes** race for 3-year-olds, running the 1 1/2-mile distance in 2:29 2/5. Second place goes to "Tide Rips" with "Tailspin" finishing third in the historic stakes race that was first run in 1867. The winner receives $78,900. **31**

1947 Packard Super Touring Sedan

1947 Norge Appliances (Far Left) "Ro-Ta-Tor" Washer (Left) Home Oil Heater (Right) Divided-Top Gas Range

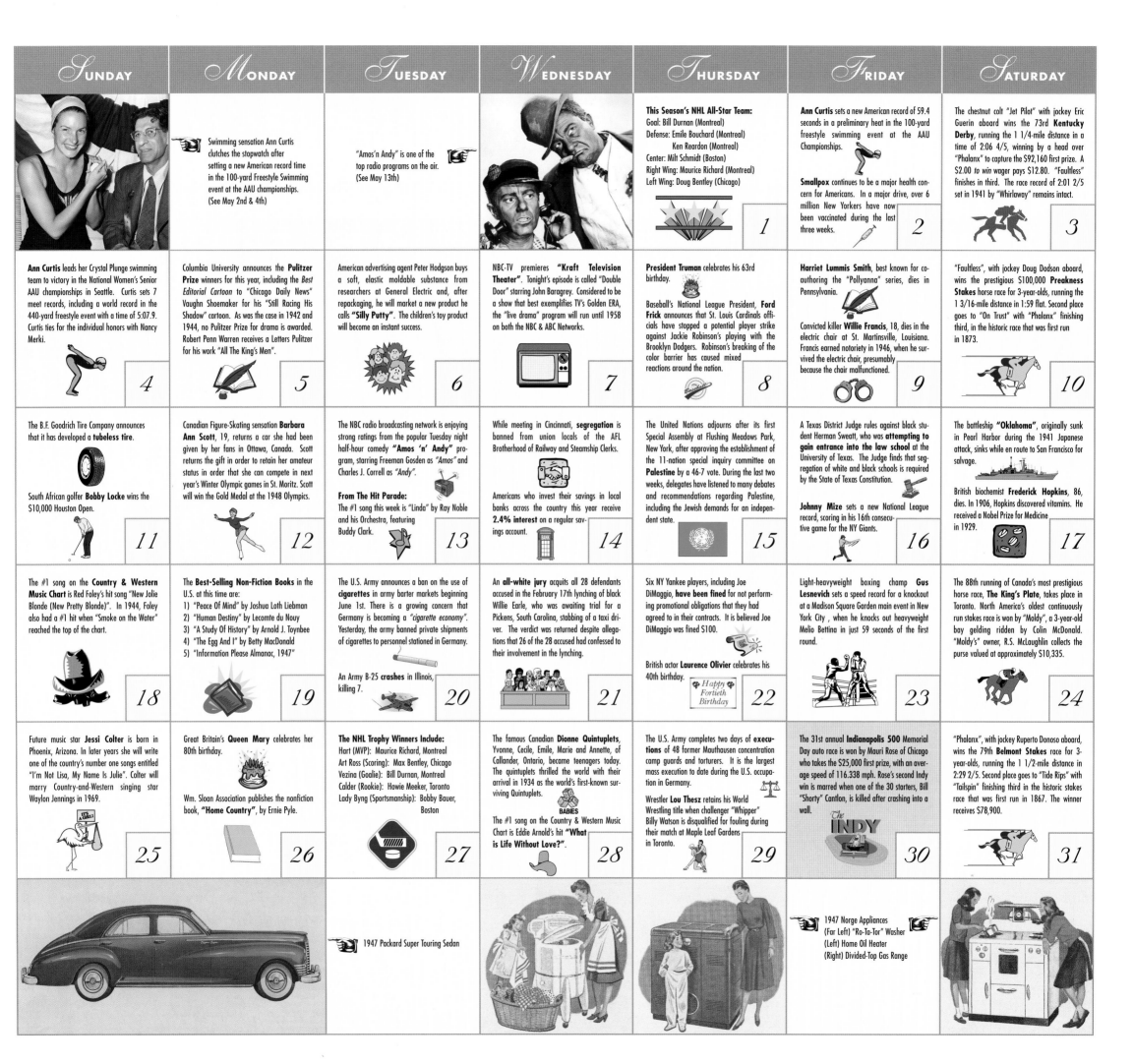

Edmund Gwenn, Natalie Wood and Maureen O'Hara star in the new film "Miracle On 34th Street".

Sunday 1

NBC-Radio premieres **"The Jack Parr Show"** as a summertime replacement for its ever popular "Jack Benny Show". Parr will earn nationwide fame from 1957 to 1962 as the host of television's "Tonight Show".

Actress **Marilyn Monroe** celebrates her 21st birthday.

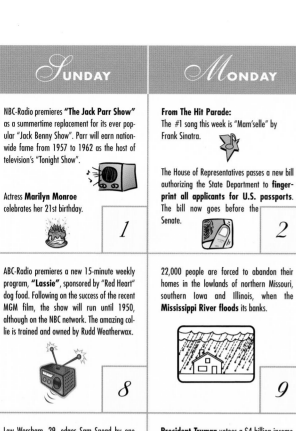

Monday 2

From The Hit Parade:
The #1 song this week is "Mam'selle" by Frank Sinatra.

The House of Representatives passes a new bill authorizing the State Department to **finger-print all applicants for U.S. passports**. The bill now goes before the Senate.

Tuesday 3

British Prime Minister Clement Attlee announces a British plan to **partition British India** into two Indias - an independent Moslem state called "Pakistan" and a Hindu state called "Hindustani". The plan, accepted by Sikhs, Moslems and Hindus, is well-received. Hundreds have died during civil war-like confrontations.

Wednesday 4

The Canadian freighter **"Emperor"** sinks in Lake Superior near Fort William, Ontario, taking 12 crew members, including 3 women, to their deaths.

Harper Publishing releases the fiction book **"The Moonlight"**, by Joyce Cary.

Thursday 5

U.S. Secretary of State George C. Marshall presents a plan for the **economic recovery of Europe** during a speech at Harvard. The detailed plan is not recognized by the Soviet Union or its satellites who will choose not to attend a July conference designed to finalize the plan.

Friday 6

It is widely reported that **newspaper columnist Lee Martimer** has dropped his **assault charge** against entertainer Frank Sinatra after agreeing to a $9,000 out-of-court settlement.

Saturday 7

The #1 song this week on the **Country & Western Music Chart** is Bob Wills' hit "Sugar Moon". In 1946, Wills had two #1 hits with "White Cross On Okinawa" and "New Spanish Two-Step".

A severe **tornado** strikes Sharon, Pennsylvania, and Youngstown, Ohio, killing 5 people.

Sunday 8

ABC-Radio premieres a new 15-minute weekly program, **"Lassie"**, sponsored by "Red Heart" dog food. Following on the success of the recent MGM film, the show will run until 1950, although on the NBC network. The amazing collie is trained and owned by Rudd Weatherwax.

Monday 9

22,000 people are forced to abandon their homes in the lowlands of northern Missouri, southern Iowa and Illinois, when the **Mississippi River floods** its banks.

Tuesday 10

From The Hit Parade:
The #1 song this week is Art Lund's version of "Mam'selle". It will remain at the top of the chart for the next two weeks.

American food shoppers can pick up a pound of **dairy-fresh butter** at local stores for the average cost of 75¢ per pound.

Wednesday 11

President Truman meets with Canadian Prime Minister King and Governor-General Viscount Alexander in Ottawa, in the **first state visit ever to Canada** by a U.S. President. President Truman makes a speech to the Canadian parliament, reasserting his doctrine of U.S. aid to "*those who seek to live at peace with their neighbors, without coercing or being coerced, without intimidating or being intimidated*".

Thursday 12

ABC-Radio introduces a new adventure program, **"The Challenge of the Yukon"**. In later years it will become better known as "Sergeant Preston of the Yukon". Created by George W. Trendle, who introduced the Lone Ranger (1933) and the Green Hornet (1938), the title role is played by Paul Sutton, aided by his wonder dog, "*Yukon King*".

Mildred "Babe" Zaharias wins the British Women's Amateur golf title.

Friday 13

A **tragic airliner accident** occurs as a Pennsylvania Central Airlines DC-4 crashes in Virginia, en route to Washington from Chicago during a heavy rainstorm. All 50 people aboard are killed.

Saturday 14

The #1 song on the Country & Western Music Chart is **"It's A Sin"** by Eddy Arnold. It is his 2nd hit of this year.

An American Medical Association meeting in Atlantic City reports that surgery remains the only cure for **cancer** victims. It is estimated that up to 98% of all stomach cancer victims will die from the disease.

Sunday 15

Lew Worsham, 29, edges Sam Snead by one stroke in a play-off to win the **47th U.S. Open Golf Championship** at the St. Louis Golf Club in Missouri. Snead once again has let the Open slip away from him. He could have tied the playoff on the 18th hole but missed a 30-inch putt. Little does he know that he will never win the Open during his otherwise sensational golf career.

Monday 16

President Truman vetoes a $4-billion income-tax reduction bill, saying "it is not the right kind of tax reduction at the right time".

Government officials order railroads to **install automatic safety devices** on all tracks on which trains exceed 60 mph.

Tuesday 17

NBC-Radio introduces the detective stories of Raymond Chandler in **"The Adventures of Philip Marlowe"**. "Marlowe" is played by Van Heflin. The summer series will run for 14 shows on NBC before being picked up by CBS on September 26th, 1948, when Gerald Mohr assumes the role of "Marlowe". Tonight's show is called "Redwing".

Wednesday 18

The Harvard rowing team wins America's oldest intercollegiate athletic event, the **Yale-Harvard rowing race**, to take a 43-39 edge in the prestigious 82nd-year event.

At home, Cincinnati Reds pitcher Ewell Blackwell, 24, tosses Major League Baseball's first **"no-hitter"** of the season in a 6-0 shutout over the Boston Braves.

Thursday 19

American Army Air Force Colonel **Albert Boyd**, 40, makes flying history as he takes his jet-propelled Lockheed P-80R to a speed of 632.8 mph over the Muroc Air Field in California.

Friday 20

From The Hit Parade:
The #1 song this week is "Peg O' My Heart" by The Harmonicats. It will remain on top of the charts for 8 weeks. Other versions of this song by Buddy Clark and The Three Sons will also reach the top of the charts.

Saturday 21

Illinois track star **Herb McKinley** breaks the 440-yard world record with a time of 46.2 seconds. The 220-yard low hurdles world record also falls when Harrison Dillard races the distance in 22.3 seconds.

"Assault", ridden by Eddie Arcaro, wins the **Brooklyn Handicap** at Aqueduct, New York, becoming the all-time money winner with $576,670.

Sunday 22

Marking the 6th anniversary of the **German invasion** of Russia in 1941, Moscow officials broadcast a radio proclamation that the "*Soviets could have won World War II unaided!*"

Bobby Riggs wins the **National Professional Tennis Championship** over Don Budge in Forest Hills, New York.

Monday 23

CBS-Radio debuts a new program, **"Wendy Warren and the News"**. The serial includes a real 3-minute newscast to open the show, read by Douglas Edwards.

Future actress Meredith Baxter and actor Michael Gross are born. Ironically, in future years the two will be paired as husband and wife on the hit TV show **"Family Ties"**.

Tuesday 24

The 29th **Professional Golf Association (PGA) Championship** is won by Jim Ferrier, 32, over Chick Harbert, 2 & 1, at Plum Hollow Golf Club in Michigan. The PGA was first formed in 1916. Ferrier was born in Australia in 1915.

Wednesday 25

Boxer **Jimmy Doyle**, 22, of Los Angeles, who was knocked out yesterday by champ Sugar Ray Robinson during a World Welterweight boxing title fight in Cleveland, dies after suffering a cerebral hemorrhage.

Thursday 26

George Seaton directs the heartwarming story **"Miracle On 34th Street"** about a Macy's Store employee named "Kris Kringle" who thinks he is the real "Santa Claus". The movie stars Edmund Gwenn, Maureen O'Hara, John Payne, Gene Lockhart, Natalie Wood, Porter Hall, William Frawley and Jerome Cowan. Edmund Gwenn will win an Oscar for "*Best Supporting Actor*".

Friday 27

The **first pension plan** for the automobile industry is granted by Ford Motors to the UAW at a cost of $200 million initially and then $15 million yearly. Ford workers also receive a 7¢-per-hour increase.

Saturday 28

From The Hit Parade:
The #1 song this week is "Chi-Baba, Chi-Baba (My Bambino Go To Sleep)" by Perry Como.

William Holden, Joan Caulfield, Billy DeWolfe, Edward Arnold and Mona Freeman star in **"Dear Ruth"**, a wartime romantic comedy film released by Paramount.

Sunday 29

President Truman addresses a NAACP convention in Washington, pledging to have the nation's government "*defend the rights and equalities of all Americans*".

1946 runner-up Betty Jameson wins the 2nd **U.S. Women's Open Golf** championship by 6 strokes over Sally Sessions and Polly Riley in North Carolina.

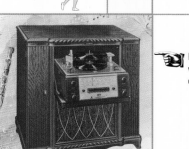

Monday 30

The Pan-American Constellation Clipper "America" lands in New York, completing the first **globe-circling commercial flight** in 13 days (4 days, 5 hours flying time). A group of U.S. publishers travelled the 25,003-mile route, touching down in Newfoundland, Eire, London, Istanbul, Karachi, Calcutta, Bangkok, Manila, Shanghai, Nanking, Tokyo, Guam, Wake, Honolulu, San Francisco and Chicago.

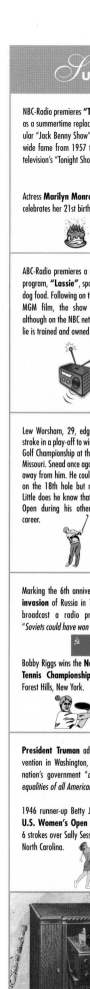

 RCA Victor's "The Crestwood" with newly-designed record-changer and FM radio.

 Runner-up Don Budge congratulates champion Bobby Riggs after losing a 5-set marathon at the National Professional Tennis Championships. (See June 22nd)

 Betty Jameson wins the Women's U.S. Open Golf Championship. (See June 29th)

Roller skating to big band music is a popular pastime.

LET THIS BE A LESSON TO YOU!
WEATHER-BIRD SHOES

TUESDAY 1

Girls' shoes from Weather-Bird are great in all sorts of bad weather.

Severe damage in excess of $12 million is experienced in the St. Louis area as the **Mississippi River** reaches its highest crest in over 100 years. Governors call for the President to declare the most affected areas to be disaster zones.

WEDNESDAY 2

Americans across the country are listening to the music of **Red Ingle** and the Natural Seven with his hit song "Temptation (Tim-Tayshun)".

THURSDAY 3

Mutual-Radio premieres **"Voyage of the Scarlet Queen"**, starring Elliot Lewis as Capt. Philip Carney. Each week's 30-minute show takes the listener on a port-to-port voyage. Tonight's voyage is the "Shanghai Secret" from San Francisco to Honolulu.

Peter Lorre hosts a new 30-minute mystery-horror radio show **"Mystery in the Air"**.

FRIDAY 4

Major League Baseball Standings:
NL: Brooklyn holds a 1-game lead over Boston
AL: New York is 7 1/2 games up on Detroit and Philadelphia

A United Airlines crew witnesses nine **flying saucer-type discs** during a flight over Emmett, Idaho. The discs are reported by hundreds of witnesses, but the Air Force calls them a "weather phenomenon".

SATURDAY 5

At the all-England tennis tournament at **Wimbledon**, Margaret Osborne defeats fellow American Doris Hart 6-2, 6-4 to win the Women's title. Jack Kramer earlier won the Men's crown 6-1, 6-3, 6-2 over fellow-American Tom Brown.

The first black baseball player to play in the American League makes history as **Larry Dolby** joins the Cleveland Indians.

SUNDAY 6

ABC-Radio premieres **"The Candid Microphone"** hosted by Allen Funt. The show is the forerunner to a new TV show, "Candid Camera" that will debut in August of 1948.

From The Hit Parade:
The #1 song is "Peg O' My Heart" by Buddy Clark with the Mitchell Ayres Orchestra.

MONDAY 7

"Tired of the everyday grind? Ever dream of a life of romantic adventure? Want to get away from it all? We offer you **"Escape"**! William Conrad's gripping voice booms out over the CBS airwaves to introduce the new radio show featuring spine-tingling tales from such masters as Joseph Conrad, Arthur Conan Doyle and Edgar Allen Poe.

TUESDAY 8

At Chicago's Wrigley Field, the 14th annual Major League Baseball **All-Star Game** is won by the American League team which edges the National League 2-1. NY Yankees pitcher Frank Shea records the win.

Headlines in a Roswell, New Mexico, paper report the existence of a crashed **flying saucer.**

WEDNESDAY 9

Britain's King George VI and Queen Elizabeth proudly announce the engagement of their daughter, **Princess Elizabeth** Windsor, 21, to Lt. Philip Mountbatten, 26, the former Prince of Greece, who has known his future bride since early childhood.

Future Football star **O.J. Simpson** is born in San Francisco, California.

THURSDAY 10

The 2nd Major League Baseball *no-hitter* of the season is registered by pitcher Don Black, 29, of the Cleveland Indians, in a 3-0 no-hit shutout over the Philadelphia Athletics.

Future folk singer **Arlo Guthrie** is born in Brooklyn, New York.

FRIDAY 11

University of California scientists successfully complete the first extensive **smashing of an atom** by use of a man-made machine. Utilizing a 4,000-ton cyclotron and 200 million electron volts, the scientists report freeing as many as 30 nuclear particles in just one bombardment.

SATURDAY 12

A popular activity on a Saturday night for teenagers is to go to the local **roller rink** and skate to Big Band Music played over loudspeakers.

The Broadway play **"Life With Father"** closes after an all-time record of 3,213 performances, surpassing the previous mark of 3,182 set by "Tobacco Road". The play which premiered on November 8th, 1939, has grossed in excess of $10 million.
BROADWAY

SUNDAY 13

The **Top-Selling fiction books** in the U.S. at this time are:
1) "Gentlemen's Agreement" by Laura Hobson
2) "Kingsblood Royal" by Sinclair Lewis
3) "The Vixens" by Frank Yerby
4) "The Big Sky" by A.B. Guthrie
5) "There Was A Time" by Taylor Caldwell

The two-week World Encampment of **Girl Scouts** in Pennsylvania comes to a close.

MONDAY 14

The Mark II Programmable Computer begins giving erroneous information. Investigations by Navy personnel will discover a dead moth next to a faulty relay. In a log, it is noted "first actual bug found". The term "computer bug" will become synonymous with finding program problems.

TUESDAY 15

The **Paris Economic Recovery Plan Conference** for Europe ends its four-day session with the 16 national representatives appointing a committee that will estimate that a four-year European recovery program would require $22.4 billion in aid. The Soviet Union chooses not to participate.

"Mammy" composer **Walter Donaldson**, 54, dies in California of a liver disease.

WEDNESDAY 16

Rocky Graziano, in front of 18,547 spectators in Chicago Stadium, becomes the new World Middleweight Boxing Champion as he knocks out Tony Zale at 2:10 of the 6th round. Graziano comes back to win after he is knocked down in the 3rd round by Zale who has been the champ since 1941.

THURSDAY 17

Scotland's Deborah Kerr stars in her first American film, **"The Hucksters"**, with Clark Gable, Sydney Greenstreet, Adolphe Menjou, Ava Gardner, Keenan Wynn and Edward Arnold. Directed by Jack Conway, the movie is released by Metro-Goldwyn-Mayer.

FRIDAY 18

President Truman signs the important **Presidential Succession Act** which designates the Speaker of the House and the President pro tempore of the Senate as the next in succession after the President, should the situation arise.

Kenneth C. Royale succeeds Robert P. Patterson as **Secretary of War**.

SATURDAY 19

The Hooperatings of the **top radio programs** during this summer include:
1) "Walter Winchell"
2) "Crime Doctor"
3) "Take It Or Leave It"
4) "Mr. District Attorney"

Illinois University announces that it will manufacture a **tuberculosis vaccine** for nationwide distribution at a cost of 1/2¢ a dose.

SUNDAY 20

Future rock star **Carlos Santana** is born in Autlan de Navarro, Mexico. Santana will become lead singer and guitarist of the rock group Santana. Their first two albums, "Santana" and "Abraxas" will become very successful, including hit singles "Oye Como Va" and "Evil Way".

The **NFL** rules no team can sign a player with college eligibility left.

MONDAY 21

Baseball's **Hall of Fame** in Cooperstown, New York, honors:
Jesse Burkett   Frank Chance
Jack Chesbro   Mickey Cochrane
Johnny Evers   Clark Griffith
Lefty Grove   Carl Hubbell
Frank Frisch   Joe Tinker
Tom McCarthy   Joe McGinnity
Eddie Plank   Rube Waddell
Ed Walsh

TUESDAY 22

Bizarre weather strikes the midwestern U.S. as the city of **Cleveland is hit by a snowstorm!** The city of Chicago records a record low temperature for this date of 49°F.

The #1 song this week on the **Country & Western Music Chart** is "Smoke! Smoke! Smoke! (That Cigarette)" by Tex Williams.

WEDNESDAY 23

President Truman makes a surprise visit to **Capitol Hill**, the first such visit by a President since 1789. The former senator from Missouri takes advantage of an opportunity to sit in his former Senate seat.

The recently-released fiction book **"Prince of Foxes"** by Samuel Shellabarger is selling briskly in the U.S. It will go on to sell over 2.4 million copies.

THURSDAY 24

Cary Grant, Myrna Loy, Shirley Temple, Rudy Vallee and Harry Davenport star in the RKO Radio release, **"The Bachelor and the Bobby-Soxer"**. The screenplay is by Sidney Sheldon and the movie's director is Irving Reis.
ADMIT ONE

FRIDAY 25

American Suffrage leader and founder of the National Birth Control League, **Mrs. Mary Ware Dennett**, 75, dies in New York.

Norwegian-born University of Minnesota star Fortune Gordien sets a **world discus record** in Oslo, Norway, tossing the disc 178.47 feet.

SATURDAY 26

President Harry Truman's mother, **Mrs. Martha Truman**, 94, dies in Grandview, Missouri after having suffered failing health during the last year. She passes away shortly after 11pm as the President is en route from Washington to be with her. Truman's father, John Anderson, died in 1914.

SUNDAY 27

The first session of the **80th Congress** ends when the Senate adjourns until January 6th, 1948. Final bills cleared to the White House by the Senate include an investigation into high prices on consumer goods by the Joint Economic Report Committee, and an approval of agreement to establish a permanent U.N. Headquarters on an East River, Manhattan, site in New York City.

MONDAY 28

The Senate War Investigating Committee opens hearings into the Government's $18-million contract with Howard Hughes and Henry Kaiser to develop a **flying boat**. The 200-ton flying boat has never been flown. A subpoena will be issued July 31st for Hughes to appear before the committee but he will avoid it saying he will appear August 6th as planned.

TUESDAY 29

A Harrisburg, Virginia, **beauty shop** suddenly explodes, killing ten women. An estimated thirty others are injured in the blast.

An insane ex-soldier leads police on a murderous chase in the RKO Radio film, **"Crossfire"**, starring Robert Young, Robert Mitchum, Robert Ryan, Gloria Grahame, Paul Kelly and Sam Levene.

WEDNESDAY 30

According to the well-respected Hooperatings list of summer radio shows, the most-listened-to evening program is **Walter Winchell's "Journal"** which has been on the air since 1932. The popular newspaper columnist, a fast-talking, brash and nervy personality, is estimated to have 20 million listeners to his 15-minute shows.

THURSDAY 31

A **fire sweeps through a French prison** killing 22 women inmates.

Stanford University researchers announce they have **developed a polio vaccine** that has been successful in experiments with rats. The researchers stop short of discussing whether the vaccine will protect humans.

Deborah Kerr makes her American film debut in the new film "The Hucksters". (See July 17th)

Clark Gable, Ava Gardner and Edward Arnold star in the new film "The Hucksters". (See July 17th)

Cary Grant and 19-year-old Shirley Temple star in the new film "The Bachelor and The Bobby-Soxer". (See July 24th)

Bill Odom, piloting the "Reynolds Bombshell", receives a hero's welcome after his "Round-The-World" flight.

Sunday	Monday	Tuesday	Wednesday	Thursday	Friday	Saturday

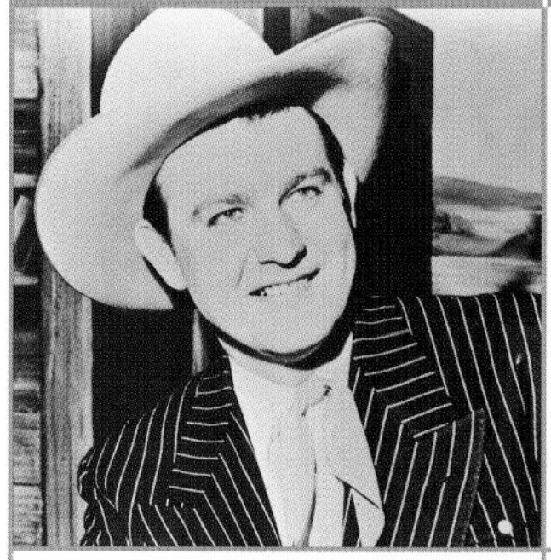

Country & Western star Tex Williams has the #1 song with his hit "Smoke! Smoke! Smoke! (That Cigarette)".
(See August 11th)

1947 Ford with 4-ring aluminum pistons. "There's A Future In Your Future".
(See August 17th)

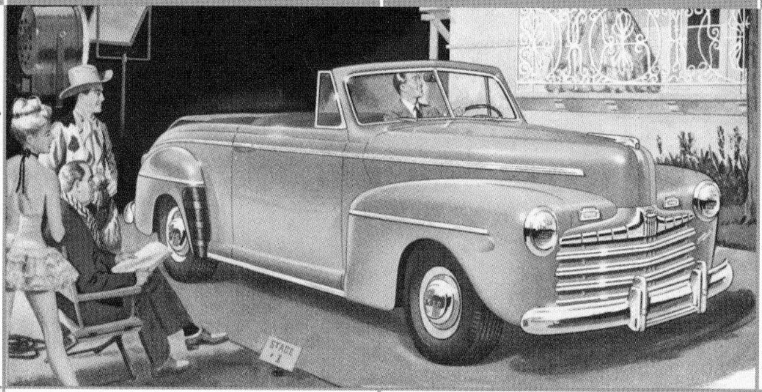

1
The University of Nebraska Museum announces that it has found the 1-million-year-old **fossilized bones** of a marsupial, saber-toothed tiger-like animal near Cambridge, Nebraska.

2
Millions of Americans listen to the widely-acclaimed **"Your Hit Parade"** radio program, which is now in its 14th year. The popular NBC program counts down the top songs in the Hit Parade around the nation, climaxing at the show's conclusion with the playing of the current #1 song.

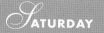

3
From The Hit Parade:
1) "Peg O' My Heart" Al Bryan and Fred Fisher
2) "That's My Desire" Helmey Kresa and Carroll Loveday
3) "I Wonder, I Wonder" Daryl Hutchins
4) "Across The Alley From The Alamo" Joe Green
5) "Chi-Baba Chi-Baba" Al Hoffman, Mack David and Jerry Livingston

4
Ike Williams becomes the undisputed World Lightweight Boxing Champion when he knocks out Bob Montgomery during the 6th round of their bout in Philadelphia. Montgomery will retire from boxing on December 26th.

5
The **Packard Motor Car Company** announces it is raising car prices by up to $200 to account for increased prices of parts and metals.

AUTO INDUSTRY

The British Ocean Liner **"Queen Mary"** arrives in New York, completing its first postwar voyage.

6
It was exactly two years ago today that an **atomic bomb was released** from a U.S. B-29 bomber over Hiroshima. Three days later another atomic bomb was dropped on Nagasaki. Japan surrendered 3 weeks later.

Howard Hughes, 41, makes his first public appearance before the Senate War Investigating Committee.

7
After nearly 15 weeks and more than 4,000 miles, the **Kon-Tiki** Pacific raft expedition comes to an end on the Raroia reef, Tuamoto Archipelago. Lead by Thor Heyerdahl, 32, the balsa raft set out from Peru seeking to prove that the pre-Incan Indians from South America could have settled in the Polynesian Islands.

8
One of the most popular radio shows during this summer is **"Dr. I.Q."**, hosted by Lew Valentine. During the NBC radio show, the host awards cash prizes to contestants for correctly answered questions, but when they are wrong, Valentine consoles his guest with *"I'm sooo sorry - give a box of Doctor I.Q. candy to that person"*.

9
The **6th World Scout Jamboree** gets underway in Moisson, France, with 32,000 Scouts from 38 countries in attendance. This includes 1,151 scouts from the United States. There are now a record 2.1 million Boy Scouts in the United States as Scouting enjoys its largest popularity ever.

10
Bill Odom, 27, successfully completes his solo around-the-world flight in 73 hours, 5 minutes, 11 seconds. Odom left Chicago and averaged 335 mph, to erase the previous record he set in April and the solo record of Wiley Post, who took 186 hours and 49 minutes during 1933.

11
Bill Odom, along with his wife and sponsor Milton Reynolds, rides through the streets of Chicago during a hero's welcome-home celebration.

The #1 song on the **Country & Western Music Chart** this week is "Smoke! Smoke! Smoke! (That Cigarette)" by Tex Williams.

12
According to government sources, more Americans are **eating meat** as a regular part of their diet than at any other time in U.S. history. The average cost of a Porterhouse steak $1 per lb.

13
The film **"Black Narcissus"**, written, produced and directed by Michael Powells, opens in New York City. It stars Deborah Kerr, Sabu, Flora Robson and David Farrar. The New York film critics will cite Kerr for *Best Performance* for her role.

ADMIT ONE

14
Golfer **Mrs. Mildred "Babe" Didrikson Zaharias**, 32, gives up her amateur status to accept $300,000 to make a series of golf movies. Mrs. Zaharias was selected by an AP poll as the *Outstanding Woman Athlete of the Year* in both 1945 and 1946.

15
After 346 years, British rule comes to an end as the **Indian subcontinent** achieves independence. The area is divided into two zones - India the Hindu state and Pakistan the Moslem state. Both nations join the British Commonwealth as dominions. Mohandas Gandhi is praised for his role in pushing for independence during the last 30 years.

16
Warner Brothers releases the film **"Life with Father"**. Adapted from the record-breaking Broadway play, the movie stars William Powell, Irene Dunne, Jimmy Lydon, Martin Milner and 15-year-old Elizabeth Taylor.

A Billboard poll picks **"All My Sons"** as *Best Play* of 1946-1947, while "Finian's Rainbow" is *Best Musical*.

BROADWAY

17
Kenneth Holmboe, 15, of Charleston, West Virginia, captures the 10th annual **All-American Soap Box Derby** Championship in Akron, Ohio, as he defeats 135 other contestants. This year's celebrity guests include Air Force Gen. James H. Doolittle and movie star Jimmy Stewart.

18
The **Hewlett-Packard Co.** incorporates in California. Over the years Hewlett-Packard will produce more than 10,000 products worldwide, including computers and systems, calculators and measuring instruments, to name just a few. During the 1980's, Hewlett-Packard will be considered by many to be one of America's best-managed firms.

19
Red Barber announces the first CBS-TV telecast of a Major League Baseball contest between the Brooklyn Dodgers and the Cincinnati Reds.

Actress **Greek Garson**, 36, files divorce papers against husband Richard Ney, 34. Ironically, Ney had played her son in "Mrs. Miniver".

20
Commander Turner Caldwell Jr. sets a **new world speed record** over Muroc Lake, California, as he races his D-558 Skystreak Navy jet plane to 640.7 mph. The achievement will not last long, however, as Marine Maj. Marion Carl, in the same plane, will set a new mark at 650.6 mph just 5 days from now.

21
The film biography **"The Roosevelt Story"**, composed of scenes from newsreels and library film covering 40 years, opens in New York City.

22
Willie Pep retains his World Featherweight Boxing title when he knocks out Jock Leslie in 45 seconds of the second round in Flint, Michigan.

For the first time in the 14-year history of the "Chicago Tribune's" annual football classic, the **College All-Stars** upset NFL Pro Chicago Bears 16-0 before 105,840 fans.

23
President Truman's daughter **Margaret Truman**, 23, makes her much-publicized concert debut in Hollywood. The soprano soloist had planned her singing debut earlier in the year but her performance was delayed due to laryngitis.

24
The **U.S. National Safety Council** reports that traffic accidents are the 4th highest cause of death following heart disease, cancer, and brain hemorrhages. Of 99,000 accidents last year, over 33,000 deaths were as a result of traffic fatalities.

25
Ford Motor Co. raises prices $86 to $299. The new price ranges are:
Mercurys: $1,490-$2,075
Lincolns: $2,390-$4,460
Luxury Models: $1,780-$2,150

Norton Publishing releases the fiction novel **"The Garretson Chronicle"**, by Gerald Warner Brace.

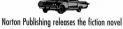

26
For the first time, passengers on both the Ohio and Baltimore Railroad trains are able to place commercial **telephone calls** while en route between New York City and Washington D.C. It is one of the first steps towards mobile telephones.

Dan Bankhead, 26, of the Brooklyn Dodgers becomes the first black to pitch in the major leagues.

27
20th Century-Fox releases **"Kiss Of Death"**, starring Victor Mature, Brian Donlevy, Coleen Gray and Richard Widmark.

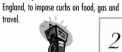

ADMIT ONE

Postwar pressures force officials in London, England, to impose curbs on food, gas and travel.

28
Spain's most famous bullfighter **Manuel "Manolete" Rodriguez**, 30, dies from shock and loss of blood after being gored by a bull. Rodriguez had recently returned to the ring following a brief retirement when adoring fans had pressured him into returning. The nation goes into a period of national mourning.

29
Pan American Airlines begins its first scheduled nonstop flights between New York and London.

Future tennis great **Robert Charles Lutz** is born in Lancaster, Pennsylvania.

30
From The Hit Parade:
The #1 song this week is "Near You" by Francis Craig and his Orchestra. It will remain in the top spot for 17 weeks until Vaughn Moore replaces it with "Ballerina".

31
Inflation continues to be one of America's most important issues as government sources indicate record prices for the second straight month. A $10 purchase of groceries in 1935 now costs $29.30 for the same items.

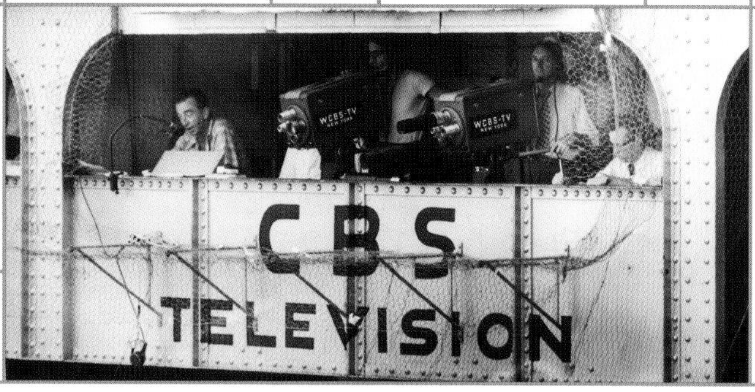

Red Barber announces the play-by-play in the first televised baseball contest on WCBS-TV for the CBS television network.
(See August 19th)

Irene Dunn, Elizabeth Taylor, 15, and William Powell star in the new film "Life With Father".
(See August 16th)

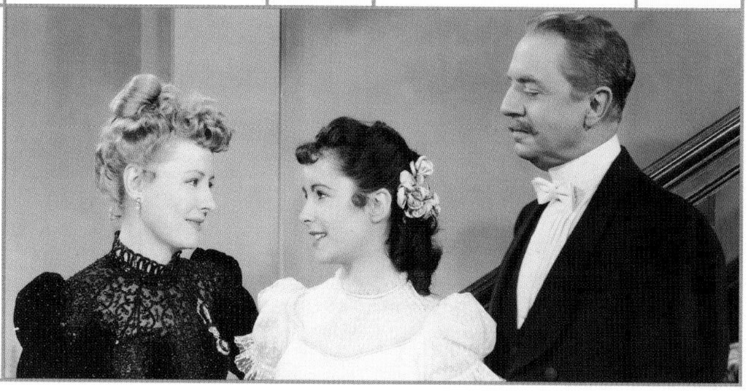

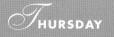

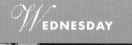

Jane Russell stars in the new Howard Hughes film "The Outlaw".

Sunday	Monday	Tuesday	Wednesday	Thursday	Friday	Saturday

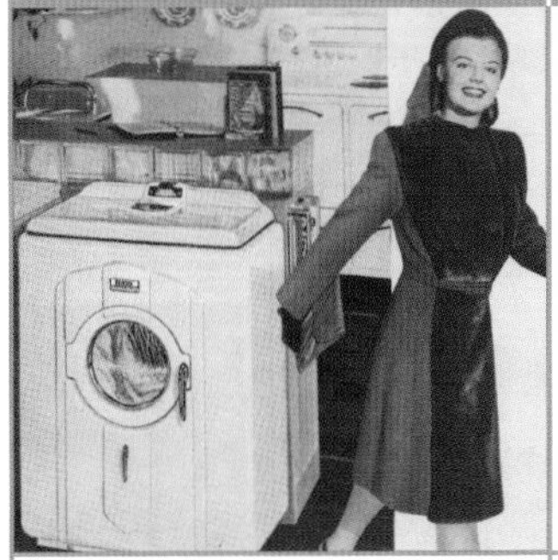

Bendix automatic home laundry.

1

The 36th International Men's Team Tennis Championship, the **Davis Cup**, is won in New York for the second consecutive year by the team from the U.S. who defeats the Australian team by the score of 4-1. The U.S. team consists of John Kramer and Ted Schroeder.

2

The Inter-American Defense Conference ends with the signing of the **Treaty of Rio de Janeiro** by 103 delegates from 19 nations. It represents a united defense against aggression. Any armed attack against an American state shall be considered as an attack against all American states.

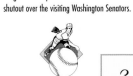

456 Americans died during the Labor Day weekend.

3

The third and last Major League baseball ***no-hitter*** to be registered during this season occurs as pitcher **Bill McCahan**, 25, of the American League Philadelphia Athletics tosses a 3-0 no-hit shutout over the visiting Washington Senators.

4

Astronomers report at their annual meeting that new evidence suggests that the **Milky Way** consists of huge red stars believed to be at least 200 million miles in diameter, which is larger than the Earth's orbit.

5

Postal rates are currently 3¢ for first-class letters, 6¢ for airmail, and 15¢ for first-class special delivery. The Post Office first began service in 1775, collecting a minimum of 6¢ to deliver a letter less than 30 miles up to a maximum of 25¢ for over 450 miles.

6

A captured **German V-2 rocket** is fired for the first time from a moving platform when the 46 foot, 14-ton rocket is launched from the aircraft carrier "Midway". The rocket travels a distance of 6 miles.

"Miss Tennessee", **Barbara Jo Walker**, 21, wins the **"Miss America"** contest in Atlantic City.

7

Despite the recent independence of India, Moslems and Hindus **continue their fierce fighting**. Officials estimate that at least 150,000 people have been killed in the Punjab which was partitioned between India and Pakistan. The Hindus have pledged to drive every Moslem out of India.

Lew Worsham wins the $15,000 Denver Open Golf event.

8

The **first helicopter service** is authorized by the Civil Aeronautics Board to the Yellow Cab Company of Cleveland.

Houghton Mifflin Publishing releases the fiction novel, **"House Divided"**, by Ben Ames Williams.

9

The current issue of **"American Magazine"** quotes former President Herbert Hoover as saying *"We would never have been attacked by the Japanese if we had not given them provocation"*. Also, agreements made with Stalin *"aren't worth a damn if they do not work out to his advantage"*. Hoover will deny making the Japanese statement on September 25th. Writer Sidney Shalett claims he quoted him correctly.

10

State Secretary **George Marshall** holds a news conference in Washington where he announces he believes the U.S. must act immediately by sending emergency food and fuel by the end of this year to Europe. Marshall forecasts severe hunger and cold conditions will exist during early 1948.

11

"The Outlaw" premieres in New York City. The film is produced and directed by Howard Hughes and stars Jane Russell, Jack Buetel, Thomas Mitchell and Walter Huston. Based on the story of "Billy The Kid", the movie was made in 1943 but has been banned until now because of its racy scenes.

12

Ralph Kiner of the Pittsburgh Pirates sets a major league record of 8 home runs in 4 consecutive games as he knocks out his 48th and 49th of the season in Pittsburgh.

Brooklyn Dodgers **Jackie Robinson** is named as baseball's *Rookie Of The Year* by the "Sporting News".

13

The 47th U.S. National Amateur Golf Championship is won by **Robert Riegel**, 2 & 1 over John Dawson at the Pebble Beach Golf and Country Club in California. A record 1,048 amateurs had entered the event.

The Broadway play **"State of the Union"** closes after 765 performances.

14

Jack Kramer makes a tremendous comeback to capture the U.S. National Tennis Championship Men's title for the second consecutive year as he defeats Frank Parker 4-6, 2-6, 6-1, 6-0, 6-3 at Forest Hills, New York. The Women's title is won by Louise Brough over Margaret Osborne 8-6, 4-6, 6-1.

The War Department decides to **black out all news** relating to biological warfare experiments.

15

The NY Yankees clinch the **American League Pennant**. The Yankees will finish the season at 97-57, 12 games ahead of second-place Detroit.

A **tidal wave** rocks Honshu, Japan, killing close to 1,800.

16

England's **John Cobb** sets a new land speed record with a combined two-run speed average of 394.196 mph at the Bonneville Salt Flats, in Utah. Cobb's fastest time of 403.135 mph is the first time the 400 mph barrier is broken.

It is revealed that **72,706 "war brides"** have now been admitted into the U.S.

17

Leading Winning Pitchers This Season:

National League
Ewell Blackwell (Cincinnati) 22-8
Lawrence Jansen (NY) 21-5
Warren Spahn (Boston) 21-10
Ralph Branca (Brooklyn) 21-12
John Sain (Boston) 21-12
American League
Bobby Feller (Cleveland) 20-11

18

Country Music history is made as singers **Ernest Tubb and Roy Acuff** perform at New York City's Carnegie Hall. This is the first country music show ever held in this venue.

Speakers at a **polio conference** in Georgia report that no preventive or cure has been found so far.

19

War veterans make use of the new **GI bill** which provides that the government will pay $1,500 for each year of university a veteran completes. Many schools are experiencing overcrowded conditions as 2.5 million students, of which half are new students, enter the schools.

Baseball star **Mel Ott** retires.

20

Fiorello Henry La Guardia, 64, dies of cancer in New York City. Best remembered as the 5'2" tall Mayor of New York from 1934-1946, he also served as a Congressman from New York from 1917-1921 and from 1923-1933.

21

Subpoenas have been issued by the House Un-American Activities Commission to 44 prominent celebrities, ordering them to appear for hearings into **Communism in Hollywood**. Some of the individuals under scrutiny are Walt Disney, Gary Cooper, Charlie Chaplin, Robert Taylor and Ronald Reagan, President of the Screen Actors Guild.

22

The **Democratic Party Rules Committee** in Georgia announces plans for the upcoming Presidential primary elections. Under the plan, blacks will vote in a separate building from white voters.

23

National League Baseball Final Standings:

	W	L	Pts
Bkln	94	60	.610
St.L.	89	65	.578
Bost.	86	68	.558
NY	81	73	.500
Cin.	73	81	.474
Chic.	69	85	.448
Phil.	62	92	.403
Pitts.	62	92	.403

24

American League Baseball Final Standings:

	W	L	Pts
NY	97	57	.630
Det.	85	69	.552
Bost.	83	71	.539
Clev.	80	74	.519
Phil.	78	76	.506
Chic.	70	84	.455
Wash.	64	90	.416
St.L.	59	95	.383

25

Awards presented at the **Cannes Film Festival** include "Dumbo" as the *Best Cartoon*, "Ziegfeld Follies of 1946" as the *Best Musical*, and "Crossfire" as *Best Social Film*.

American consumers are paying an average price of 49¢ for a **5-pound bag of sugar.**

26

New York City Baseball Commissioner **Albert Chandler** announces that the Ford Motor Co., along with the Gillette Safety Razor Co., will pay $65,000 to sponsor the first televised World Series.

Future singing sensation **Olivia Newton-John** is born in Cambridge, England.

27

Future rock star **Meat Loaf** is born under the name Marvin Lee Aday in Dallas, Texas. He will hit it big with his "Bat Out Of Hell" album.

The Walt Disney animated film **"Fun and Fancy Free"** is released by RKO Radio Pictures.

28

CBS-Radio premieres **"The Adventures of Christopher Wells"** sponsored by the Desoto Automobile Company. The show, created by Ed Byron, stars Myron McCormick.

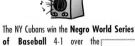

The NY Cubans win the **Negro World Series of Baseball** 4-1 over the Cleveland Buckeyes.

29

Jazz musician **Dizzy Gillespie** plays Carnegie Hall for his first concert.

A new Broadway play, **"The Heiress"** premieres in New York City. Written by Ruth & Augustus Goetz, the production stars Wendy Hiller, Peter Cookson and Basil Rathbone. It will enjoy 410 performances.

30

An estimated 3.8 million Americans watch the first **World Series televised baseball game** as the NY Yankees defeat the Brooklyn Dodgers 5-3 in game one. A five-run 5th inning clinches the Yankees win. A record 73,365 at Yankee Stadium attend the game as Frank Shed gets the win and Frank Brianco gets the loss.

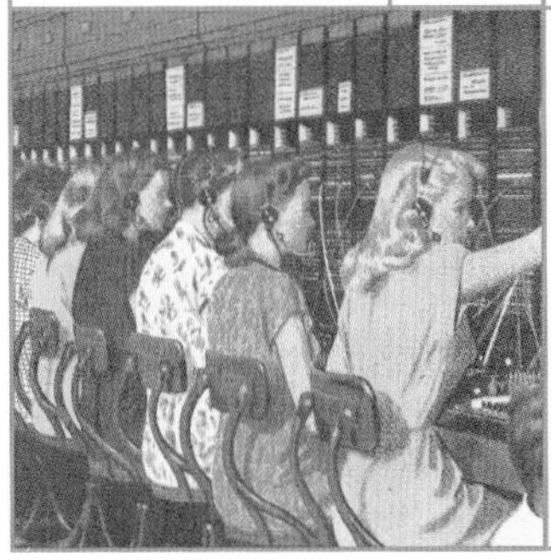

Western Electric promises "more telephone service coming for you".

New General Electric television receivers are now for sale in cities where television programs are available.

(Far Right)
The Wurlitzer 1160 rotates 24 record titles into view in 3 easy to see programs of 8 great tunes each.

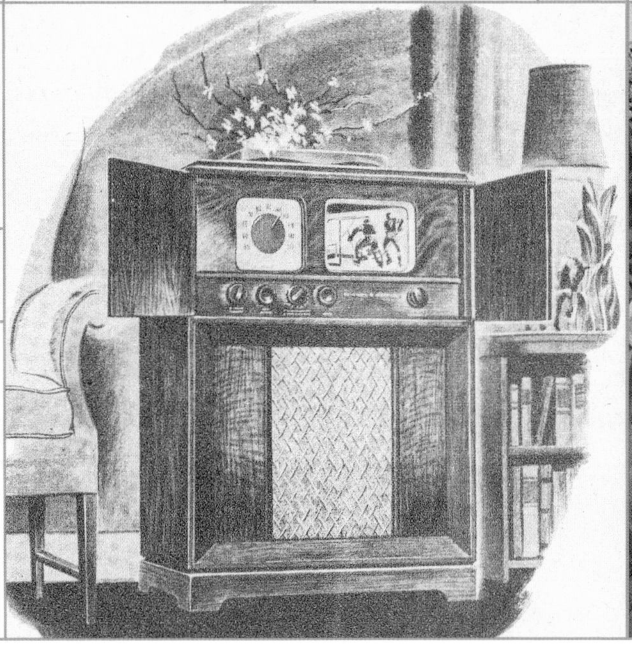

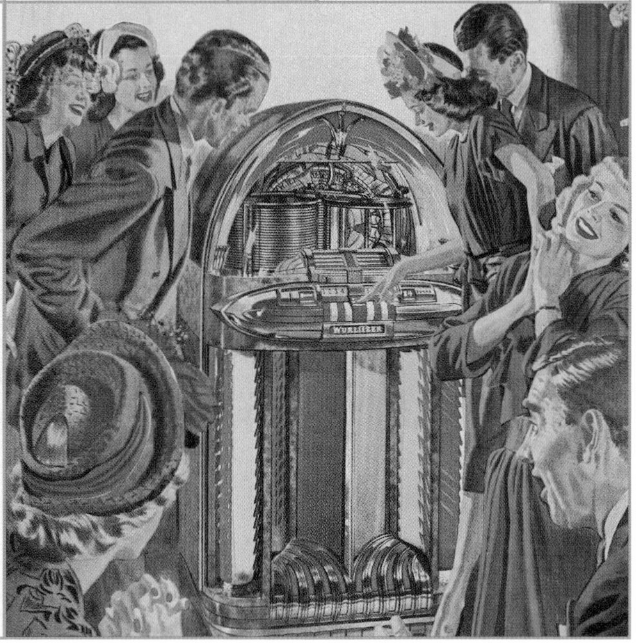

New York Yankees - 1947 World Series Champions

Sunday	Monday	Tuesday	Wednesday	Thursday	Friday	Saturday

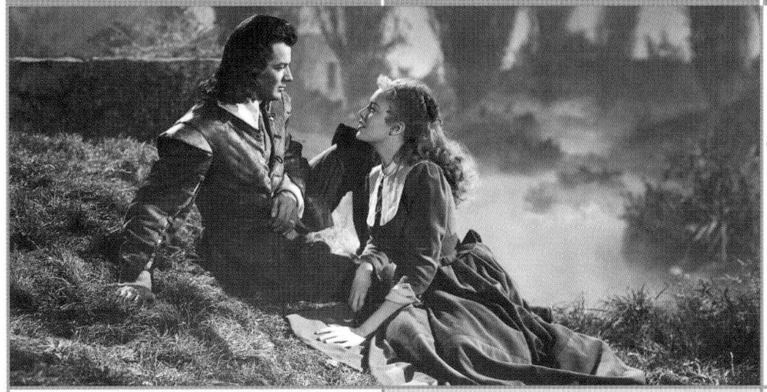

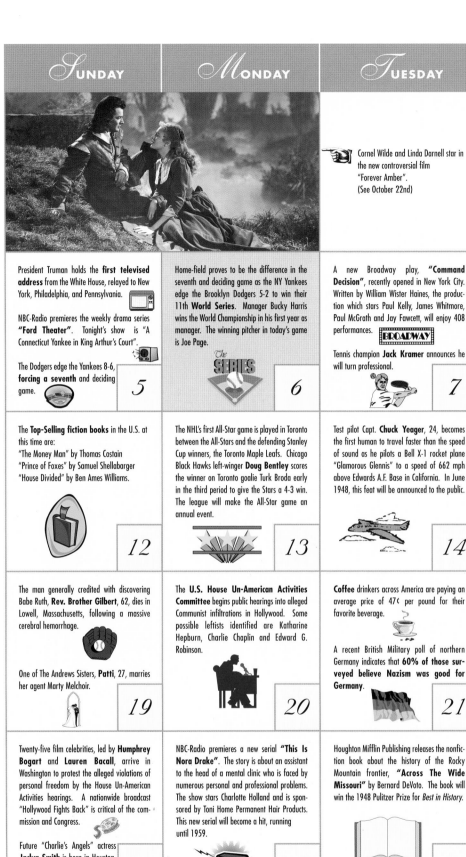

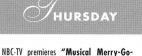

Cornel Wilde and Linda Darnell star in the new controversial film "Forever Amber". (See October 22nd)

1
The home-field **NY Yankees** defeat the Brooklyn Dodgers 10-3 to take a two-games-to-none lead in the World Series. The story of today's win rests with the Yankees' batters who pound 15 hits off four Brooklyn pitchers. Pitcher Allie Reynolds records the win.

2
NBC-TV premieres **"Musical Merry-Go-Round"**, a 20-minute live variety show hosted by Jack Kilty.

The Brooklyn Dodgers score 6 runs in the bottom of the 2nd inning and then hang on for a 9-8 win over the NY Yankees at Ebbets Field for their first victory of the series. Yankee **Yogi Berra** becomes the first pinch hitter to get a World Series home run.

3
The home-field Dodgers score a dramatic 9th-inning come-from-behind 3-2 win over the Yankees. Yankees pitcher **Bill Bevans** had a no-hitter with two out and 2 on in the 9th inning when pinch hitter Cookie Lavagetto wins the game with a hard-hit double.

4
The visiting NY Yankees edge the Dodgers 2-1. The hero for NY is right-handed pitcher **Spec Shea**, 26, who tosses a complete-game 4-hit victory. Joe DiMaggio hits his second home run of the Series.

College Football Scores:
Army 47- Colorado 0
Columbia 13 - Navy 6
North Western 27 - UCLA 26
Notre Dame 40 - Pittsburgh 6

5
President Truman holds the **first televised address** from the White House, relayed to New York, Philadelphia, and Pennsylvania.

NBC-Radio premieres the weekly drama series **"Ford Theater"**. Tonight's show is "A Connecticut Yankee in King Arthur's Court".

The Dodgers edge the Yankees 8-6, **forcing a seventh** and deciding game.

6
Home-field proves to be the difference in the seventh and deciding game as the NY Yankees edge the Brooklyn Dodgers 5-2 to win their 11th **World Series**. Manager Bucky Harris wins the World Championship in his first year as manager. The winning pitcher in today's game is Joe Page.

7
A new Broadway play, **"Command Decision"**, recently opened in New York City. Written by William Wister Haines, the production which stars Paul Kelly, James Whitmore, Paul McGrath and Jay Fawcett, will enjoy 408 performances.

Tennis champion **Jack Kramer** announces he will turn professional.

8
A new play by George Bernard Shaw, **"Man and Superman"**, opens in New York City at the Alvin Theater. The show stars Maurice Evans, Malcolm Keen, Frances Rowe, Carmen Matthews, Chester Stratton, Jack Manning and Josephine Brown. It runs for 295 performances.

9
"Herman the Mouse" and "Katnip the Cat" make their first appearance in a Famous Studios Productions cartoon episode released through Paramount Pictures entitled **"Naughty But Nice"**. Directed by Seymour Kneitel, the characters are voiced by Arnold Stang ("Herman") and Syd Raymond ("Katnip").

10
The Oscar Hammerstein and Richard Rodger's musical **"Allegro"** opens at the Majestic Theater in New York City. The large cast includes John Battles, Roberta Jonay, John Conte and Annamary Dickey. It will run for 315 performances.

11
Paramount Films releases the Cecille B. De Mille movie **"Unconquered"**. The movie, based on Neil Swanson's novel, stars Gary Cooper, Paulette Goddard, Howard Da Silva and Boris Karloff.

Betty Jameson wins the Women's Texas Open Golf title.

12
The **Top-Selling fiction books** in the U.S. at this time are:
"The Money Man" by Thomas Costain
"Prince of Foxes" by Samuel Shellabarger
"House Divided" by Ben Ames Williams.

13
The NHL's first All-Star game is played in Toronto between the All-Stars and the defending Stanley Cup winners, the Toronto Maple Leafs. Chicago Black Hawks left-winger **Doug Bentley** scores the winner on Toronto goalie Turk Broda early in the third period to give the Stars a 4-3 win. The league will make the All-Star game an annual event.

14
Test pilot Capt. **Chuck Yeager**, 24, becomes the first human to travel faster than the speed of sound as he pilots a Bell X-1 rocket plane "Glamorous Glennis" to a speed of 662 mph above Edwards A.F. Base in California. In June 1948, this feat will be announced to the public.

15
A tragedy is dramatically averted when the U.S. Coast Guard cutter "Bibb" rescues 69 passengers and crew off the Boeing **"Bermuda Sky Queen"** when it was forced down in the Atlantic Ocean yesterday en route from England. It is the first commercial passenger plane known to have ditched at sea.

16
A motion to draft **General Dwight D. Eisenhower** to run for President in 1948 gains momentum when a Washington-based group announces it has adopted the slogan *"I Like Ike"*.

17
An American citrus cooperative in Florida produces **frozen orange juice concentrate**. The juice is concentrated at 66°F by means of a heat pump then is packed frozen. The same technology will be used for other types of juices.

Actress **Rita Hayworth** celebrates her 29th birthday.

18
Ted Williams of the American League Boston Red Sox accomplished the rare "triple crown" batting feat this season with 32 home runs, 114 RBI's, and a sensational .343 average. Williams was also the last player to accomplish the rare hitting feat when he accomplished this during 1942.

19
The man generally credited with discovering Babe Ruth, **Rev. Brother Gilbert**, 62, dies in Lowell, Massachusetts, following a massive cerebral hemorrhage.

One of The Andrews Sisters, **Patti**, 27, marries her agent Marty Melchoir.

20
The **U.S. House Un-American Activities Committee** begins public hearings into alleged Communist infiltrations in Hollywood. Some possible leftists identified are Katharine Hepburn, Charlie Chaplin and Edward G. Robinson.

21
Coffee drinkers across America are paying an average price of 47¢ per pound for their favorite beverage.

A recent British Military poll of northern Germany indicates that **60% of those surveyed believe Nazism was good for Germany**.

22
20th Century-Fox releases a controversial film **"Forever Amber"**, adapted by Jerome Cady from the novel by Kathleen Winsor and directed by Otto Preminger. Cardinal Francis Spellman and the Catholic Legion of Decency condemn the film, but the first days receipts at the Roxy Theater in New York City are a record $25,308.

23
President of the Screen Actors Guild, **Ronald Reagan** testifies in Washington as part of the ongoing House Committee on Un-American Activities. Reagan testifies that the Actors Guild is not controlled by "leftists".

24
President Truman addresses the nation by radio in a special televised broadcast, explaining why he has called for an **emergency session of Congress** for mid-November. Truman's concern focuses on inflation which is rising at 16% a year. Food costs are up 40% since 1946.

25
Forest fires sweep through thousands of acres of timberland in Maine, forcing President Truman to declare the state a disaster area. Seventeen deaths are reported, along with an estimated $30 million in damages including Bar Harbor, which is partially destroyed.

26
Twenty-five film celebrities, led by **Humphrey Bogart** and **Lauren Bacall**, arrive in Washington to protest the alleged violations of personal freedom by the House Un-American Activities hearings. A nationwide broadcast "Hollywood Fights Back" is critical of the commission and Congress.

Future "Charlie's Angels" actress **Jaclyn Smith** is born in Houston, Texas.

27
NBC-Radio premieres a new serial **"This Is Nora Drake"**. The story is about an assistant to the head of a mental clinic who is faced by numerous personal and professional problems. The show stars Charlotte Holland and is sponsored by Toni Home Permanent Hair Products. This new serial will become a hit, running until 1959.

28
Houghton Mifflin Publishing releases the nonfiction book about the history of the Rocky Mountain frontier, **"Across The Wide Missouri"** by Bernard DeVoto. The book will win the 1948 Pulitzer Prize for *Best in History*.

29
The play, **"The Winslow Boy"**, opens at the Empire Theater in New York City, staged by Glen Byam Shaw, and starring Michael Newell, Alan Webb, Valerie White and Frank Allenby. It will win the N.Y. Drama Critics Circle award for *Best Import*.

Future actor **Richard Dreyfuss** is born in Brooklyn, New York.

30
The **Best-Selling Nonfiction Books** in the U.S. at this time are:
"Inside U.S.A." by John Gunther
"Peace of Mind" by Joshua Loth Liebman
"A Study of History" by Arnold Toynbee

31
The **Nobel Peace Prize** is awarded this year to the American Friends (Quakers) Service and the British Society of Friends Service Council for their humanitarian contributions.

California Institute of Technology officials announce that corn grown from seeds which were exposed at the recent Bikini Atomic Blast, shows **major abnormalities** in the second generation.

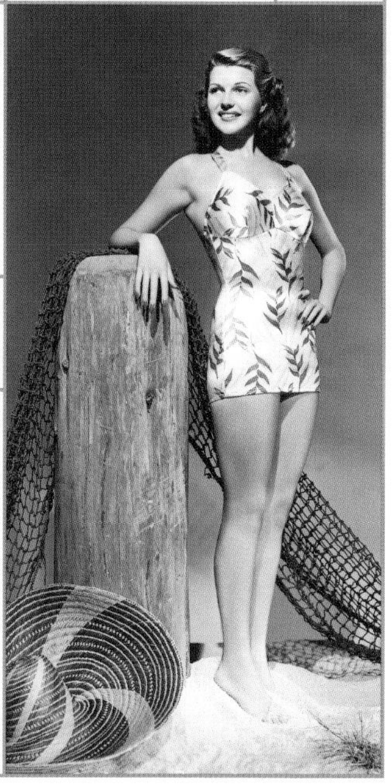

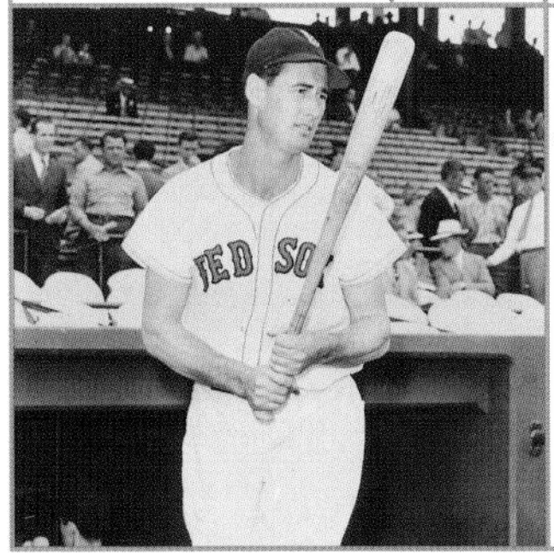

Boston Red Sox star Ted Williams accomplishes a rare Triple Crown Batting Title. (See October 18th)

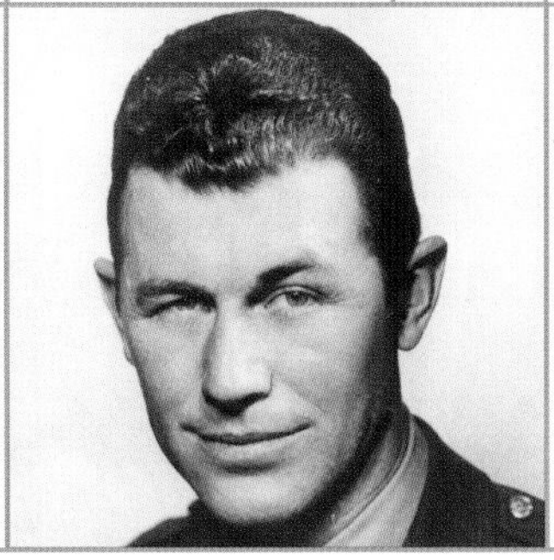

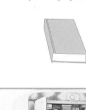

Test pilot Chuck Yeager, 24, becomes the first to break the sound barrier in his plane "Glamorous Glennis". (See October 14th)

Get the best things first... Get Kelvinator.

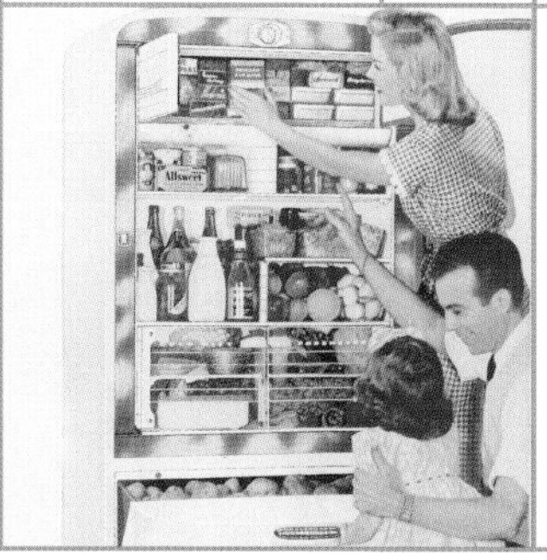

Actress Rita Hayworth celebrates her 29th birthday. (See October 17th & November 13th)

TIME · PASSAGES

NOVEMBER *1947*

Gregory Peck, Dorothy McGuire and John Garfield star in the new film "Gentleman's Agreement".

Sunday	Monday	Tuesday	Wednesday	Thursday	Friday	Saturday

Howard Hughes at the controls of the 200-ton, eight-story-tall flying boat the "Spruce Goose".
(See November 2nd)

NX37602

Heir to the British throne, Princess Elizabeth, 21, marries Philip Mountbatten, 26, at Westminster Abbey.
(See November 20th)

1

One of America's greatest racing thoroughbreds **"Man O' War"** dies at the age of 30. Owned by Sam Riddle, the horse dominated racing during 1919-21, winning 20 of 21 races, capturing a record $200,000 in prize money.

The #1 song on the **Country & Western Music Chart** is "I'll Hold You In My Heart (Till I Can Hold You In My Arms)" by Eddy Arnold.

2

Thousands crowd into the Long Beach Harbor in California to watch the world's largest airplane, Howard Hughes' **"Spruce Goose"**, rise 70 feet in the air. The $25-million "flying boat" weighs 200 tons.

The 7th **Ryder Cup** golf title is won by the U.S. team (captained by Ben Hogan) 11-1 over Great Britain.

3

An American **War Crimes Court** in Nuremberg, Germany, announces 4 former S.S. leaders are to die by hanging for their World War II crimes: Heinrich Himmler, Maj. Karl Somner, Col. Franz Eirensch Malz, and Maj. Gen. George Loerner. Eleven others are sentenced to prison terms ranging in length from 10 years to life.

4

A new play by F. Hugh Herbert, **"For The Love of Money"** opens in New York City at Henry Miller's, starring June Lockhart, John Loder, Vicki Cummings, Mark O'Daniels and Grover Burgess. The show will run for 263 performances.

BROADWAY

5

The NHL **Chicago Black Hawks** recently traded the league's leading scorer Max Bentley and rookie Cyril Thomas to the Toronto Maple Leafs for Gus Bodnar, Gaye Stewart, Bob Goldham, Bob Poile and Ernie Dickens. Fans in both Chicago and Toronto have mixed reactions to the trade.

6

MGM Motion Pictures releases the film **"Cass Timberlane"**, starring Spencer Tracy, Lana Turner, Zachary Scott and Mary Astor. Directed by George Sidney, the film is based on the best-selling book by Sinclair Lewis.

ADMIT ONE

7

The average cost of purchasing **precious metals** during this year is $35 for an ounce of gold and 72¢ for an ounce of silver. On September 29th, a world record gold price was set in Manila at $48.40 an ounce.

8

Consumers purchasing a loaf of **white bread** are paying an average price of 13¢ at supermarkets across the nation.

College Football Scores:
Notre Dame 27 - Army 7
Ohio State 7 - Northwestern 6
Princeton 33 - Harvard 7
Wisconsin 46 - Iowa 14

9

Consumers are using a new aerosol food product, aerated whipped cream from **Reddi-Whip**. This is the first major U.S. aerosol food product.

Willie Hoppe retains his world 3-cushion billiards title, defeating Arthur Rubin in Perth Amboy, N.J.

10

Actress **Rita Hayworth**, 29, divorces **Orson Welles**, 32, in Los Angeles.

The **Johnson & Johnson Company** celebrates its 60th anniversary.

A Box Office popularity poll picks **Ingrid Bergman and Bing Crosby** as the most popular movie stars.

11

20th Century-Fox releases the Darryl F. Zanuck film production **"Gentlemen's Agreement"**, directed by Elia Kazan and starring Gregory Peck, Dorothy McGuire, John Garfield, June Havoc and Celeste Holm. The movie will win Oscars for *"Best Picture"*, *"Best Director"*, and *"Best Supporting Actress"* for Celeste Holm.

12

A **total eclipse of the Sun** is witnessed in Hawaii. Americans on the west coast view a partial eclipse.

Tennis great **Jack Kramer** turns professional, signing a $50,000-a-year contract.

13

Rita Hayworth, the beautiful and talented actress, is the cover picture in this week's "Life Magazine". This is Hayworth's fourth appearance on the front cover of the popular weekly publication.

A Nobel Prize for Physics is awarded to **Sir Edward Appleton**, 55, of Great Britain for his discovery of the Appleton Layer which reflects radio short waves in the ionosphere.

14

Billy Fox, 22, wins a TKO in the 4th round over light-heavyweight boxing title contender Jake La Motta, 26, in New York City.

15

The Air Force announces that the world's first **Ram Jet helicopter** built by McDonnell Aircraft has been successfully test-flown. The "Flying Bike" can fly at 50 mph and weighs 310 pounds.

College Football Scores:
Notre Dame 26 - Northwestern 19
Illinois 18 - Ohio State 7
Princeton 17- Yale 0
Michigan State 14 - Temple 6

16

Pan American Airlines ground workers are awarded a 19¢-per-hour wage increase by a board of New York arbitrators.

American smokers are paying an average price of 17¢ per pack of **cigarettes**.

17

President Truman addresses the reconvened **80th Congress** in Washington. Truman urges the immediate adoption of a $597-million aid program for Europe's Italy, France and Austria. Truman then outlines a 10-point program to halt inflation, including wage and price controls.

18

Communist-led riots in Italy have resulted in the deaths of at least 22 people during a week of heavy violence. At least 200 people were injured as over 100 anti-Communists clubs are destroyed. Premier Alcide de Gasperi accuses the Communists of trying to interfere with U.S. aid.

19

CBS-TV premieres a daytime series, **"Missus Goes A Shopping"**, hosted by John Reed King in a live program where audience members go shopping at a variety of Manhattan, New York, supermarkets.

Whittlesey House Publishing releases the fiction novel **"The Tamarack Tree"**, by Howard Breslin. The historical novel will win the Literary Guild selection for December.

20

The future Queen of England, **Princess Elizabeth**, 21, marries **Philip Mountbatten**, 26, in a Westminster Abbey wedding ceremony which is broadcast and televised all over the world. Prince Philip's three sisters were not invited to the wedding since they married German Princes.

21

A U.S. Navy Neptune **patrol plane crashes** off the coast near San Diego, taking nine lives. Two men manage to survive the crash.

The N.Y. State Athletic Commission **suspends boxer Jake La Motta** for concealing an injury prior to his recent fight against Bill Fox which he lost.

22

A quart of **fresh milk** delivered to homes across the country costs an average of 20¢ which is the highest price since 1919.

The **first electric guitar** is used publicly by Merle Travis who had asked Paul Bigsby to design one for him. In 1948, Leo Fender will introduce a new line of electric guitars marketed as the "Broadcaster".

23

The first **inter-racial football game** is held in the south as the black Willow Tree Athletic Club and the white Alpine Athletic Club battle to a 6-6 tie before a "non-segregated" crowd in Durham, South Carolina.

The **Campbell Soup Company** celebrates its 25th anniversary.

24

Viking Publishers releases **"The Pearl"** by John Steinbeck. The fiction work retails for $2.

The Cleveland Indians sign shortstop **Lou Boudreau** as manager for two more seasons. (The Indians will win the 1948 World Series)

25

Relenting to political pressures, the American Motion Picture Co. votes to bar 10 screenwriters suspected as Communists, thereby, in effect, **blacklisting** the writers. The industry pledges not to employ them until they declare under oath that they are not Communists.

26

A revival of Shakespeare's **"Anthony and Cleopatra"** opens in New York City at the Martin Beck Theater. Presented by Katharine Cornell, the play stars Miss Cornell, Godfrey Tearle, Kent Smith, Lenore Ulrich, Joseph Holland and Ralph Clanton.

BROADWAY

27

Americans celebrate another **Thanksgiving** in peace. Many gather with family and friends to give thanks for the bountiful harvest. Others enjoy football as the Chicago Bears pound the home-field Detroit Lions 34-14.

28

The Major League Baseball **Most Valuable Player awards**, selected by the Baseball Writers Association, go to outfielder Joe DiMaggio of the American League NY Yankees for the third time, and to third-baseman Bob Elliott of the National League Boston Braves.

29

The United Nations votes 33-17 in the General Assembly in favor of portioning the **Holy Land** into two independent Jewish and Arab states by October 1st, 1948. Following the vote, six Arab delegations walk out proclaiming they will not be bound by the decision.

College Football Scores:
Army 21 - Navy 0

30

NBC-Radio's **"Your Hit Parade's"** lists its most popular songs:
1) "Near You" by Kermit Goell & Francis Craig
2) "You Do" by Mack Gordon & Joe Myrow
3) "I Wish I Didn't Love You So" by Frank Loesser
4) "And Mimi" by Jimmy Kennedy & Nat Simon

SEE 'EM PUFF SMOKE!
HEAR 'EM "CHOO-CHOO

American Flyer Trains:

(Top)
New York Central Freight with remote control and 140" oval track $39.95.

(Bottom)
Pennsylvania Freight with remote control and 120" oval track just $129.95.

Spencer Tracy, Cameron Mitchell and Lana Turner star in the new film "Cass Timberline".
(See November 6th)

Tennessee Williams' play "A Streetcar Named Desire", starring Marlon Brando and Jessica Tandy, opens in New York City.

Sunday	Monday	Tuesday	Wednesday	Thursday	Friday	Saturday

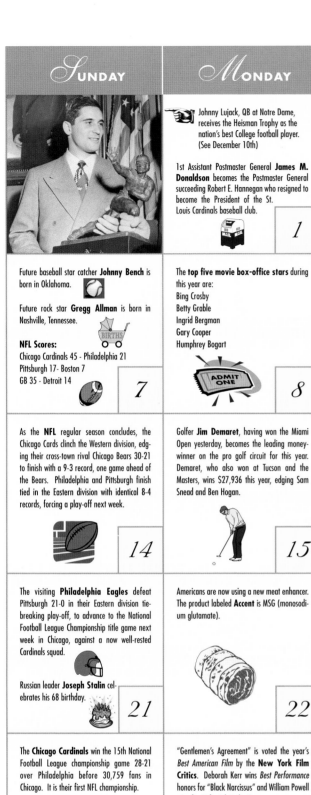

Monday 1: Johnny Lujack, QB at Notre Dame, receives the Heisman Trophy as the nation's best College football player. (See December 10th)

1st Assistant Postmaster General **James M. Donaldson** becomes the Postmaster General succeeding Robert E. Hannegan who resigned to become the President of the St. Louis Cardinals baseball club. — **1**

Tuesday 2: Women's World Tennis Rankings:
1) Margaret Osborne (U.S.A.)
2) Louise Brough (U.S.A.)
3) Doris Hart (U.S.A.)

Men's World's Tennis Rankings:
1) Jack Kramer (U.S.A.)
2) Ted Schroeder (U.S.A.)
3) Frank Parker (U.S.A.) — **2**

Wednesday 3: "A Streetcar Named Desire", by Tennessee Williams, opens at the Barrymore Theater in New York City, starring Jessica Tandy, Marlon Brando, Karl Malden and Kim Hunter. The play will run for 855 performances. Staged by Elia Kazan, the production will win the 1948 Pulitzer Prize for *Best Play* and will also win the New York Critics *Best Play* Award. — BROADWAY — **3**

Thursday 4: The AP & UP joint selections All-American Football Team for this year includes:
QB: John Lujack - Notre Dame
Backs: Doak Walker - SMU
Robert Chappius - Michigan
Center: Charles Bednarik - Penn St.
End: Bill Swiacki - Columbia — **4**

Friday 5: World Heavyweight Boxing Champ **Joe Louis** wins an unpopular 15-round split decision over Jersey Joe Walcott as the 10-1 underdog knocks Louis down twice. It is Louis' 24th defense of his title during the last 10 years.

A federal grand jury in Washington indicts the **Hollywood 10** for not declaring to the sub-committee whether or not they are Communists. — **5**

Saturday 6: President Truman dedicates the new **Everglades National Park** in Everglades City, Florida.

Brooklyn Dodgers coach **Leo "The Lip" Durocher**, who was suspended on April 9th, is reinstated replacing Burt Shotton. — **6**

Sunday 7: Future baseball star catcher **Johnny Bench** is born in Oklahoma.

Future rock star **Gregg Allman** is born in Nashville, Tennessee.

NFL Scores:
Chicago Cardinals 45 - Philadelphia 21
Pittsburgh 17 - Boston 7
GB 35 - Detroit 14 — **7**

Monday 8: The **top five movie box-office stars** during this year are:
Bing Crosby
Betty Grable
Ingrid Bergman
Gary Cooper
Humphrey Bogart — **8**

Tuesday 9: RKO Radio releases the Samuel Goldwyn film **"The Bishop's Wife"**, starring Cary Grant, Loretta Young and David Niven.

Columbia University announces **General Dwight D. Eisenhower** will assume the Presidency of their University. — **9**

Wednesday 10: The Heisman Memorial Trophy, awarded annually to the nation's best college football star, is presented to **Johnny Lujack**, the sensational quarterback for Notre Dame. Lujack led his team to championships in 1946 and 1947, and played on all four Varsity squads. — **10**

Thursday 11: The musical revue **"Angel In The Wings"** opens in New York City with sketches by Hank Ladd, Ted Luce and Grace & Paul Hartman. Words & music are by Bob Hilliard and Carl Sigman. The show will run for 308 performances. BROADWAY

An **Army C-47 crashes** at the Memphis, Tennessee, Airport killing 20 people. — **11**

Friday 12: From The Hit Parade:
The #1 song is "Ballerina" by Vaughn Monroe. The song will remain in the top spot for ten weeks.

The highest-paid film stars in the United States during this year are Humphrey Bogart at $467,000 and Bette Davis at $328,000. — **12**

Saturday 13: This season's AP All-Pro Football Team includes:
Backs: Sid Luckman - Chicago Bears
Otto Graham - Cleveland
Steve Van Buren - Philadelphia
Orban "Spec" Sanders - NY
Center: Clyde Turner - Chicago Bears — **13**

Sunday 14: As the NFL regular season concludes, the Chicago Cards clinch the Western division, edging their cross-town rival Chicago Bears 30-21 to finish with a 9-3 record, one game ahead of the Bears. Philadelphia and Pittsburgh finish tied in the Eastern division with identical 8-4 records, forcing a play-off next week. — **14**

Monday 15: Golfer **Jim Demaret**, having won the Miami Open yesterday, becomes the leading money-winner on the pro golf circuit for this year. Demaret, who also won at Tucson and the Masters, wins $27,936 this year, edging Sam Snead and Ben Hogan. — **15**

Tuesday 16: The **average annual wage** per working person in the U.S. for this year is $2,602.

An **Army B-29 Superfortress crashes** in Arizona killing twelve people. — **16**

Wednesday 17: Oklahoma faith healer **Oral Roberts**, 29, is now broadcasting his ministry over two radio stations. By 1960, his ministry will have over 2 million members.  — **17**

Thursday 18: Future film director **Steven Spielberg** is born in Cincinnati, Ohio. Spielberg will go on to a phenomenal career, directing numerous hit movies including "Jaws", "Close Encounters of the Third Kind", "E.T." and "Schindler's List". — **18**

Friday 19: World Welterweight Boxing Champion **Sugar Ray Robinson**, in his second defense of his title, knocks out fellow-American Chuck Taylor during the 6th round of their bout in Detroit, Michigan. — **19**

Saturday 20: Brothers-in-law Burton "Butch" Baskin and Irvine Robbins have merged their small chain of ice cream stores in southern California. Beginning in 1948, **Baskin & Robbins** plan to franchise their stores that offer over 100 different ice cream flavors. — **20**

Sunday 21: The visiting **Philadelphia Eagles** defeat Pittsburgh 21-0 in their Eastern division tie-breaking play-off, to advance to the National Football League Championship title game next week in Chicago, against a now well-rested Cardinals squad.

Russian leader **Joseph Stalin** celebrates his 68 birthday. — **21**

Monday 22: Americans are now using a new meat enhancer. The product labeled **Accent** is MSG (monosodium glutamate). — **22**

Tuesday 23: Lopert Films releases the French film **"Beauty and the Beast"**, an adult imaginative interpretation of the children's classic starring Jean Marais, Josette Day, Marcel Andre and Mila Parely.

President Truman **grants pardons to 1,523 men** convicted during World War II of violating the Selective Service Act. All but 3 of the men pardoned have served time in jail. — **23**

Wednesday 24: "Time Magazine" has selected George C. Marshall for the second time for *Man Of The Year*. The Commander was also selected by "Time" for the honor in 1943. — **24**

Thursday 25: Warner Brothers releases the film **"The Voice of the Turtle"** starring Ronald Reagan, Eleanor Parker and Eve Arden.

RKO Motion Pictures releases the film **"The Fugitive"**, directed by John Ford and starring Henry Fonda and Dolores Del Rio. — **25**

Friday 26: New York City is brought to a virtual standstill when a **snowstorm** dumps a record 25 inches of snow in 16 hours. It is the heaviest snowfall to hit New York City since 1888. Other cities including Boston, Philadelphia and areas of Connecticut also receive heavy snow. Officials estimate 55 people have died as a result of the severe snowstorm. — **26**

Saturday 27: NBC-TV premieres **"Puppet Playhouse"** starring Bob Smith and his marionette friend "Howdy Doody". The show will become a hit in 1948 when it will become known as "Howdy Doody" with Bob Smith ("Buffalo Bob"). — **27**

Sunday 28: The **Chicago Cardinals** win the 15th National Football League championship game 28-21 over Philadelphia before 30,759 fans in Chicago. It is their first NFL championship.

"Ring Magazine's" *Fighter Of The Year* is Light-Heavyweight Champion **Gus Lesnevich**. — **28**

Monday 29: "Gentlemen's Agreement" is voted the year's *Best American Film* by the **New York Film Critics**. Deborah Kerr wins *Best Performance* honors for "Black Narcissus" and William Powell wins for "Life with Father".  — **29**

Tuesday 30: The **Hooper Ratings Poll** of radio favorites:
1) Fibber McGee and Molly
2) Jack Benny
3) Fred Allen
4) Charlie McCarthy
5) Radio Theater
6) Red Skelton
7) Amos 'N' Andy
8) Bob Hope — **30**

Wednesday 31: The AAU James E. Sullivan Memorial Trophy for the outstanding amateur athlete goes to sculls champion **John B. Kelly Jr.**

King of the Cowboys, **Roy Rogers** marries **Dale Evans** in Davis, Oklahoma.

The **population** of the United States is estimated to be 144.2 million. — **31**

Bing Crosby, star of "Philco Radio Time" Wednesday nights on ABC, enjoys the new sensational Philco 1201 record player and radio.

Henry Fonda and Dolores Del Rio star in the new film "The Fugitive". (See December 25th)

1947 Dodge